·汉英对照·

马德五 编著　潘智勇 绘

世界图书出版公司
上海·西安·北京·广州

图书在版编目（CIP）数据

孔子说／马德五编著；潘智勇绘.—上海：上海世界图书出版公司，2004.1
ISBN 7-5062-6234-7

Ⅰ.孔... Ⅱ.①马...②潘... Ⅲ.①儒家②论语-译文—汉、英 Ⅳ.B222.24

中国版本图书馆CIP数据核字（2003）090448号

孔子说（汉英对照）

马德五编著 潘智勇绘

上海世界图书出版公司 出版发行
上海市尚文路185号B楼
邮政编码 200010
上海艺炎美术设计有限公司设计排版
上海欧阳印刷厂印刷
各地新华书店经销

开本：889×1194 1/24 印张：12.5 字数：398 000
2004年1月第1版 2004年1月第1次印刷
印数 1-6 000
ISBN 7-5062-6234-7/H・463
定价：25.00元

孔子说

◎目录

CONTENTS

# 前言

## 学而时习之，不亦说乎？

20世纪80年代，当我还住在怀俄明州时，有一次与家人去西雅图旅游，在中国街一家中国书店内买到了一本中英文对照《四书》，一时如获至宝。从此以后，每当有暇时就会将书拿出来阅读。慢慢地我发现了译者James Legge原来是一百多年前的英国来华传教士。他的维多利亚式的英文，典雅有之，清新流利则嫌不足。

1996年底，我搬到休士顿后，有一天，我在华侨文教服务中心图书馆内又发现了两本中英文对照《论语》，一本是台湾的侨务委员会印发，另一本是台北市政府印送的。惟这两本书的译者是同一个人——清末民初的辜鸿铭先生。辜前辈一生梳着一条大辫子，喜欢闻女人的裹脚布。他主张一夫多妻就像一个茶壶配有多只茶杯一样。我发现他的《论语》英译和他的为人一样，读来也是怪怪的，因而不敢苟同。

于是，我开始下定决心，将《论语》重新译成尽可能像美国口语一样的英文，以使当今美国读者易于了解孔子当年究竟说了哪些话。

我的英文译本已于2001年由美国印第安纳州的First Book Library公司出版。书名就叫做Confucius Said(《孔子说》)。现再以中英文对照方式出版，除了英文和原来的文言文外，又加上我的白话文翻译，同时更有潘智勇先生的插图，将孔子的形象以画笔一一勾画了出来，以补我文字上的不足，方便国人研读。

# 英文版序言

## PREFACE OF THE ENGLISH VERSION

上世纪60年代初，当我以一个外国学生身份初来美国时，我时或听到一些引用的话语说是孔子说的。我以一个台湾大学中国文学系毕业生的身份告诉我的美国朋友们，据我所知，孔子从未说过这些话语。于是他们问我孔子说过些什么话。真是大哉问也！

When I first came to the United States in the early 1960s as a foreign student, I sometimes heard quotations which were said to be the words of Confucius. Being a graduate of Taiwan University, majoring in Chinese literature, I told my American friends that, as far as I knew, Confucius had never said those words. I was then asked what Confucius had said. That was indeed a big question!

40年后的今天，我来回答这个问题。

Let me answer this question today, four decades later.

孔子学说绝对不是如同基督教或佛教一样是一种宗教。可是它对整个中国文化的影响决不亚于基督教之于西方或佛教之于东方。孔子在中国以及东南亚国家的历史中是如此悠久及狂热地被崇拜，东方人可真的尊敬他几乎把他当作一位宗教的创始人了。因此，在当今世界上犯罪率和混乱不断上升时，全世界都在提倡孔学之研究。孔子学说真有这个能力去解决每个人的困难吗？在10世纪初中国宋朝一位有名的宰相赵普曾经说过，如果他的官员们都能读熟和实践即使是半部《论语》的话，他的国家就会大治及繁荣起来的。

Definitely, Confucianism is not a religion like Christianity or Buddhism, but its influence in the whole Chinese culture is not less than that of Christianity in the West or Buddhism in the East. Confucius has been so long and so fervently worshiped in China, as well as the Southeastern Asian nations, that the Oriental people are truly respecting and treating him nearly as a founder of religion. Amid the increasing rate of crime and chaos, the world is now paying more attention to the studies of Confucianism. Could Confucius really have the ability to solve everyone's problems? One of the famous Chinese prime ministers in the Song Dynasty in early tenth century, Zhao Pu, declared that if all his offcials could memorize and carry out only half of the *The Analects of Confucius*, his nation would be prosperous and in very good order.

如欲明了孔子究竟是怎么样的一个人及他的信念是什么，我们应当先从他的一生来看。

In order to understand who Confucius was, and what he believed, we should start with his life.

孔子在公元前551年出生于鲁国，即在当今中国的山东省境内。那个时候，西周王朝下面的很多小国不断发生战争。因为西周王朝的天子已经无力统治这个庞大的帝国，只好让那些小国一代一代地相互争伐。

Confucius was born in 551 B.C. In a nation called Lu, in the present Province of Shandong, China. This was at a time of constant warfare among many small nations in the Chinese mainland under the Western Zhou Dynasty. The emperor of Western Zhou Dynasty could not rule his huge kingdom very well, so his small nations fought among themselves.

孔子生于一个平民家中。在那个时代里，只有贵族的子弟才有机会去接受学校教育。虽然如此，孔子仍是利用每一个机会去研读经典及学习有用的技能。他相信每三个人中之一人一定知道一些其他两个人所不知道的事理，所以他经常向别人学习。孔子是如此地勤奋好学，所以在不过三十多岁时，他就已经成为鲁国境内一位有名望的学者了。

Confucius was from an ordinary family with the last name of Kong. During those days, only the noble families' children had the opportunities to go to school. However, Confucius used every opportunity to study classical books and learn useful skills. He believed that every one of three people would know something which the other two did not know, so he often learned from others. He was so diligent in learning things, that by his early 30s, he had become a well known scholar in the nation of Lu.

孔子34岁时，他所出生的国家鲁国发生政治混乱。他率领一批弟子逃到北方的邻国齐国去，很快地便受到齐国国君的尊敬。孔子在齐国住了八年后又回到他的出生地鲁国。数年后，他终于有机会被鲁国国君任命为司寇。这是他第一次也是最后一次有机会施展他的政治抱负。

When he was 34, Lu, the nation in which he was born, was in great political chaos. He took a group of disciples, fleeing to the northern nation, Qi, and immediately received high respect from the king of Qi. Confucius stayed in Qi for eight years then returned to his birth place, Lu. A few years later, he finally had an opportunity to be appointed by his king as a senior official. It was his first and only time to put his political philosophy into practice.

三年后，孔子被免职，开始周游列国。在往后的14年中，他一共住过六个国家。他一直希望能再有机会去施展他的政治理念，可他再也没有如愿，终其余生以教导学生为职业，成为中国最伟大的教师。

After being discharged three years later, he started to tour around just about all the nations in China. He had stayed in six nations in fourteen years. He kept hoping to have another chance to practice his political philosophy again, but he never had. He spent the rest of his life in teaching. Finally, he became the greatest teacher in China.

他说只要有人能够付他一点点象征性的学费，他就不会拒绝教导这个人。他是中国第一位开办学校的平民，而且不管学生是来自贵族或是平民，他都接受。因此，与其说孔子是一位伟大的政治家，毋宁说他是一位伟大的教师。史籍记载孔子曾经教过三千以上的弟子，其中有72位最为杰出。很多弟子(信徒)追随孔子一直到他逝世为止。

孔子说

He said that as long as a person could pay him a token amount of tuition, he would not turn down the person. He was the first civilian in China to open a private school and he accepted all the people, no matter whether they were noble or common citizens. Therefore, we would rather say Confucius was a deep thinker of political science, but say he was a great teacher. Records indicate that Confucius had taught more than 3,000 students. Among them, 72 were most outstanding. Many students/disciples followed Confucius until he passed away.

孔子在73岁时逝世于鲁国。很多年后，他的弟子及他们的弟子将孔子和他的一些杰出弟子的谈话记录辑成一本书，名叫《论语》，成为后来研究孔子学说的一本最具权威性的著作。

Confucius died at the age of 73 in his native nation of Lu. After his death, his students built a temple named after him. Years later, some of his students and their students compiled all of Confucius' sayings and some of his outstanding students' sayings into a book called *The Analects of Confucius* which later became the most important document used to study Confucianism.

在孔子的时代，中国处于极大的混乱中。很多有聪明才智的学者们纷纷提出各种解决方案。孔子不过是其中一位。三百多年后，公元前140年，西汉汉武帝接受了朝臣的建议，独尊儒家。理由很简单，因为孔子坚持每一个政府官员必须服从君主，而君主必须做一个好的君主。在家庭里，他认为每一个儿子必须服从父亲，而父亲也必须做一个好的父亲。如果每一个人均能如此，孔子相信，国家将会大治，犯罪率将会降低。因为每一位君主均不希望有人反叛他，孔子的学说因而自然地为历朝历代的皇帝所接受。

During Confucius's era, while China was in great chaos, there were many scholars trying hard to solve the problems. Confucius was but one of them. But some 300 years later, during Western Han Dynasty in 140 B.C., Emperor Wu taking his senior officials' advice, declared Confucianism the national political philosophy. The reason was simple because Confucius insisted that every government official must obey the emperor, while the emperor must also act as a just ruler. In the family, he urged that every son must obey his father, while the father must also act as a kind father. He believed that if everybody would practice this way, the whole nation would be in good order and few crimes would happen. As every ruler expected no rebelling against him, Confucianism was accepted naturally by every emperor in every dynasty.

6世纪末，中国隋朝的皇帝更颁布了任用官吏的考试制度，《论语》变成了主要的考试典籍之一。自此后，每一朝代均沿袭此一制度来选拔政府官吏。因此，每一位中国男子如欲参加考试，必须研读《论语》。即或有人考取并被分派一个重要的职位后，如果其行为与《论语》相抵触，该官吏仍会被政府严厉处罚。

In the late sixth century, the Chinese emperor of Sui Dynasty further proclaimed a system of examination for the employment of government officials. *The Analects of Confucius* became one of the few main textbooks to be examined. Since then, every dynasty took the system to examine their future government officials. Every Chinese man was required to the studies of *The Analects of Confucius* if he wished to become a government official. Even after a man passed the examination and held an important position in the government, if he happened to perform an action which conflicted with *The Analects of Confucius*, that particular official would still be severely punished by the government.

公元739年,唐朝玄宗皇帝又追赠孔子为"至圣先师"。政府更为孔子建庙,每一代的孔子的嫡传直系长孙可以享有公卿一般之待遇。此一优待条款一直延续下去,即使最后一个封建王朝清朝于1911年被推翻后仍然不变。孔子的73代嫡 传长孙孔德成现仍在台湾享有至圣奉侍官的尊荣。

In 739 A.D., Emperor Xuan-Zhong of the Tang Dynasty further gave Confucius an honorable posthumous title, THE GREATEST SAGE, and his government built a temple named after Confucius. Confucius' eldest direst offspring of each generation was also offered an honorable position in the central government receiving the salary and benefits almost equal to a prime minister. This kind of favorable treatment has been continuing for dynasty after dynasty even after the overthrowing of the last Chinese monarchy, Qing Dynasty, in 1911. The 73rd generation of Confucius' eldest direct offspring, De cheng Kong, still enjoys his hereditary privilege in Taiwan.

《论语》在数千年来的中国一直被视为超越任何法律的典章。任何批评都是绝对不可以的。不论在哪一个朝代或哪一位皇帝当政,即使是皇帝自己也必须尊从孔子学说的教导。此一现象,终于在1912年民国建立后而有所改变。

*The Analects of Confucius* was the most authoritative of all laws in a long Chinese history over thousands of years, and it could not be criticized, no matter in which dynsty or who the emperor was. Even the emperor himself also had to abide by the Confucius sayings. This situation finally changed when the Chinese republic was established in 1912.

孔子是伟大的,不仅因为他的政治哲学赢得中国帝王的需要,也因为他的处世哲学适合人们的需要。

Confucius is great not only because his political philosophy happened to win the ancient Chinese emperors' needs, but also because his philosophy of dealing with people meets human's needs.

孔子是一位伟大的哲学家。他相信每一个人生来都是善良的,是后天的环境把人们变得不同了。他说,"性相近也;习相远也。"孔子的一生致力于启发人性,培养品德,以谦卑真诚的态度与家人朋友及其他人相处。他特别注重仁德。他说,"德不孤,必有邻。"他最恨虚伪的语言及行为。他说,"巧言令色,鲜矣仁。"

# 孔子说

Confucius was a great philosopher. He believed that every person was good in nature. He said, "By nature, all men are nearly alike when their lives begin. When they are growing, they become different from each other because of what they practice." During all of his life, he worked hard to teach people to cultivate their minds, behave with good actions, and be humble and sincere in dealing with families, friends and all others. He emphasized virtue. He said, "A person of virtue will not be lonely, for people like to be his neighbors." He hated dishonest sayings and manners. He said, "Saying flattering words and showing flattering manners are seldom associated with virtue."

孔子是一位伟大的思想家。他要人们学习与思考并重。他说,"学而不思则罔,思而不学则殆。"他要求人们去做一件事情时只考虑事情本身的对错,如果是对的就去做,而不要一味地只想到利益。如果一个人凡事都去想如何获得利益,迟早会带来怨恨的。他说,"放于利而行,多怨。"他教导人凡是不喜欢别人对待他的,也不要将之对待别人。他说,"己所不欲,勿施于人。"

He was a great thinker. He wanted people to learn and think both. He said, "Learning without thinking is a waste, while thinking without learning is dangerous." He wanted people to go ahead working without too much thinking of getting advantage if that was a good thing. He said, "If a person wants to do everything based upon advantages he will receive, sooner or later he will receive regret in return." He taught people not to do something to the other people which he did not like the other people to do to him. He said, "What I don't want the other people to do to me, I should not do it to others."

孔子是位伟大的教师。他不管贵族或平民、富人或穷人,他都愿教。他是"有教无类。"为期教导成功,孔子认为教师自己也必须不停去学习。他说,"温故而知新,可以为师矣。"孔子教导学生如何去了解一个人。他说,"视其所以,观其所由,察其所安,人焉廋哉!"

Confucius was a great teacher. He said, "In the teaching of students, there should be not difference between the rich and the poor, or the noble and the mean." In order to teach others well, Confucius believed that the teacher himself must keep learning too. He said, "Constantly reviewing what has been acquired, and continuing to acquire new knowledge, the man may thus become a teacher." Confucius taught his students how to know a person, "If you look at a man's actions and his motives as well as what he likes, you will know what type of man he is. Then, how can he hide himself!"

虽然孔子已经在2500多年前逝世了,但他的哲学,他的教导,他的忠言,都已经深深地植入中国人的心中。数百年前,孔子的学说被传至东南亚各国,很快地就被当地人民所接受及崇拜。在早期的中国,几乎每一个城镇均有孔庙。东南亚国家也是如此。

Althought Confucius died more than 2,500 years ago, his philosophy, his teaching, and his advice, have been deeply rooted in the Chinese people's hearts. Hundreds of years ago, his doctrine was introduced into the Southeastern Asian nations and was soon accepted and worshiped as well by the people in those lands. In early times, there was a Confucius temple at every town in China And in many Southeastern nations too.

《论语》共为20章。原书最早是书写在一片片的竹简上的。时日久了,很多片竹简的次序被混乱了。因此《论语》的第一章并不就是书写在第二章前,而第二章也并不是书写在第三章前。除此以外,每一节的主题也全被乱置了。因此,在我决定将《论语》译为英文时,我将全书的章节重新编排为四章。第一章:如何做一个仁者。第二章:如何从政。第三章:孔子,一位伟大的教师。第四章:孔子,一位伟大的平民。同时,我将一些不适合当今社会需要的语句予以节略了,并将我的新书赋以新名:《孔子说》。

There are twenty chapters in *The Analects of Confucius*. The original book was written on hundreds of bamboo slices. As time went by, many bamboo slices got mixed up and lost their original order. Therefore, the first chapter may not have been written earlier than the second one, or the second chapter written earlier than the third one. Subjects were also completely mixed up. Therefore, when I decided to translate the ancient Chinese *The Analects of Confucius* into English, I reorganized the whole contents and divided them into four chapters, namely,(1) How to Be a Virtuous Man, (2) How to Be in Politics, (3) Confucius, a Great Teacher, and (4) Confucius, a Great Ordinary Man. Meanwhile, I also deleted some meaningless parts which are no longer relevant to toaday′s society. And I gave my work a new Title:*Confucius Said*.

我希望《孔子说》可以帮助西方读者了解孔子在2500多年前究竟说了些什么话。

I hope *Confucius Said* helps Western readers under stand what Confucius actually said some 2,500 years ago.

# 第一章
# CHAPTER ONE

## 如何做一个仁者
## HOW TO BE A VIRTUOUS MAN

有子曰:“其为人也孝弟,而好犯上者,鲜矣;不好犯上,而好作乱者,未之有也。孝弟也者,其为仁之本与!”

有子说:“如果一个人孝顺他的父母,尊敬他的兄长,是很少会触犯他的上级的。如果一个人不触犯他的上级是从不会为社会带来混乱的。所以说孝顺父母和尊敬兄长实在是达到仁道的基本条件啊!”

You Zi said: “If a man treats his parents with filial duty and respects his elder brothers, he will seldom offend his superiors. If a man does not offend his superiors, he will never disturb peace and order in the society. Therefore, treating parents with filial duty and respecting elder brothers should be the initial requirements of benevolence!”

子曰:“人不知而不愠,不亦君子乎!”

孔子说:“即使别人不了解他,他也不会不高兴的,那不就是君子么!”

Confucius said: “ Even though nobody understands him, he will not feel unhappy. Isn’t that a superior man!”

子曰:“巧言令色,鲜矣仁!”

孔子说:“说过分恭维的话语及呈现过分恭维脸色的人,是很少有仁德的!”

Confucius said: “Saying flattering words and showing flattering manners are seldom associated with virtue!”

曾子曰:“吾日三省吾身:为人谋而不忠乎?与朋友交而不信乎?传不习乎?”

曾子说:“我每天反省这下面三件事:为别人出主意时是否恳切?和朋友们交往时是否真诚?老师教导我的是否研习了?”

Zeng Zi said: “I judge myself on these three matters every day: Whether I was faithful when giving advices to others; whether I was sincere when dealing with friends; and whether I practiced the teachings my master taught me?”

子曰:“弟子入则孝,出则弟,谨而信,泛爱众,而亲仁。”

孔子说:“年轻人在家里应该孝顺父母;出门在外应该尊敬长者;做事应该小心信实;与人相处应该平和博爱,更要亲近仁者。”

Confucius said: “At home, a young man must treat his parents with filial duty. When he leaves home, he must respect his elders. He must be careful and faithful in doing things. When he deals with people, he must show willingness to get along with them. Furthermore, he must try to associate with the virtuous people.”

子夏曰:“贤贤易色,事父母能竭其力,事君能致其身,与朋友交言而有信,虽曰未学,吾必谓之学矣。”

子夏说:“如果一个男子娶妻只重她的品德而不去计较她的容貌,全心全力去孝顺父母,不顾一切尽力事奉国君,与朋友交往遵守信诺,虽然有人说这个人没有受过教育,可是我还是认为他是有学识的。”

Zi Xia said: “If a man can attach importance to his wife’s virtue, not her features, treat his parents with filial respect, serve his prince with all he can do, and carry out his promises when dealing with friends, I would consider him an educated man, though others may say he is uneducated.”

曾子曰:"慎终追远,民德归厚矣。"

曾子说:"当父母过世了以后,做子女的人应当恭敬地办理丧葬事宜,并祭祀祖先。如此社会二的民风便会笃厚了。"

Zeng Zi said: " When a parent passes away, children should perform the funeral rites with respect, and offer sacrifice to ancestors. In doing so, morality in society will be increased."

子曰:"君子不重则不威,学则不固。主忠信。无友不如己者。过则勿惮改。"

孔子说:"如果君子的态度不够端庄的话,他就没有威仪,同时他所学到的东西也就不会扎实。他与人相处时,他是忠诚信实的。他不结交那些不如他自己的朋友。如果他犯了过错,他是不会害怕去改正的。"

Confucius said: " If a superior man's manner is not serious, he will not get dignified bearing, and what he learnt will not be solid. He is faithful and sincere when he deals with people. He does not make friends with the people who are not as good as he is. If he makes a mistake, he won't be afraid to correct it."

子曰:“君子食无求饱,居无求安,敏于事而慎于言,就有道而正焉,可谓好学也已。”

孔子说:“君子吃饭时不会吃得太饱,居住时也不会要求太舒适的地方,工作勤奋,说话谨慎,遇到有德行的人时,就向之请教来端正自己的言行。这样的人就可以称之谓好学的人了。”

Confucius said: “When a superior man eats, he does not seek to be very full; when he lives at a house, he does not require a very comfortable one; when he works, he does diligently; when he speaks, he speaks very carefully; and when he meets a person of virtue, he learns from the person to rectify himself. Such a man is one who loves to study.”

子曰:“不患人之不己知,患不知人也。”

孔子说:“一个人不要担心别人不了解他,应当担心他不了解别人。”

Confucius said: “A person should not be concerned about nobody knowing him. He should be concerned about not knowing others.”

孟懿子问孝。
子曰:“无违。”
樊迟御。子告之曰:“孟孙问孝于我,我对曰:‘无违。’”
迟曰:“何谓也?”
子曰:“生,事之以礼;死,葬之以礼,祭之以礼。”

孟懿子问孔子孝的定义。
孔子回答:“不要违背礼。”
樊迟为孔子驾车,孔子告诉他:“孟孙问我孝的定义,我回答他:‘不要违背礼。’”
樊迟问:“这话怎么说呢?”
孔子说:“当父母在世时,应当待之以礼。在父母过世后,应当以礼安葬,以礼祭拜。”

Meng Yizi asked Confucius what the meaning of filial piety was.
Confucius answered, “Do not disobey the proprieties.”
Soon after that, when Fan Chi, a disciple of Confucius, was driving the carriage for his master, Confucius told his disciple, “When Meng Yizi asked me about filial piety, I answered him ‘Do not disobey the proprieties.’”
Fan Chi asked for explanation.
Confucius said: “While the parents are alive, the children should treat their parents according to propriety. After the parents' death, children should bury their parents and offer sacrifice according to propriety.”

子游问孝。
子曰:“今之孝者,是谓能养。至于犬马,皆能有养。不敬,何以别乎?”

子游问孔子孝的定义。
孔子说:“现在的人之所谓孝不过是养活父母而已。说起养活,我们对狗和马不也是养活么,如果没有恭敬的态度,怎么可以有所分别呢?”

Zi You also asked Confucius what the meaning of filial piety was.
Confucius answered: “The filial piety of nowadays means the support of one’s parents. As we give support to the dogs and horses as well, without reverence, what is the difference between the supports given to the parents and the animals?”

孟武伯问孝。
子曰:“父母唯其疾之忧。”

孟武伯问孔子孝的定义。
孔子说:“让父母只担心子女的疾病,其余都不用担心。”

Meng Wubo asked Confucius what the meaning of filial piety was.
Confucius answered: “Let parents worry about nothing but their children's illness.”

子夏问孝。
子曰:“色难。有事弟子服其劳,有酒食先生馔,曾是以为孝乎?”

子夏问孔子孝的定义。
孔子说:“最难的是态度。有事情时,年轻的人代劳去做,有好的食物和酒时,让年老的人去享用。这是否就足以解释孝这个问题了?”

Zi Xia asked Confucius, what the meaning of filial piety was.
Confucius answered: “The important part of filial piety is the manner. When there is something that needs to be done, the youngster will do it for his seniors. When there is food with wine, the youngster will serve his seniors first. Do these explain the subject of filial piety?”

子贡问君子。
子曰:“先行其言,而后从之。”

子贡问孔子君子的定义。
孔子说:“君子按照他想说的话去做,以后便根据他做过的去说。”

Zi Gong asked what constituted a superior man.
Confucius said: “ He acts what he plans to speak and later, he speaks according to his actions.”

子曰:“君子周而不比,小人比而不周。”

孔子说:“君子是公正而不偏心,小人是偏心而不公正。”

Confucius said: “ A superior man is impartial, not partisan; however, an inferior man is partisan, not impartial.”

子曰:"学而不思则罔,思而不学则殆。"

孔子说:"只去学习而不去思考是没有用的;只去思考而不去学习是危险的。"

Confucius said: "Learning without thinking is useless, while thinking without learning is dangerous."

子曰:"攻乎异端,斯害也矣。"

孔子说:"学习怪异的理论是危险的。"

Confucius said: " Studying strange theories is dangerous."

子曰:“非其鬼而祭之,谄也。见义不为,无勇也。”

孔子说:“如果不是他祖先的鬼魂也去祭祀的话,那就是谄媚。在义理上应当去做而不去做,那就是胆怯。”

Confucius said: “To offer sacrifice to a spirit which is not his ancestor is flattery. Not to do the right thing which he should do is cowardly.”

子曰:“人而无信,不知其可也?大车无輗,小车无軏,其何以行之哉?”

孔子说:“我不知道一个人怎么可以没有信用呢?这就好像大车子没有车軏小车子没有车驾,人们如何可以使车子行走呢?”

Confucius said: “I don’t know how could a man live without faithfulness? It is like a cart had no yoke, and a carriage had no harness. How could people make the cart and the carriage move?”

子曰:“祭如在,祭神如神在。吾不与祭,如不祭。”

孔子说:“祭祀的时候一定要认为被祭的鬼魂就好像在场一样,祭神的时候也要当神祇在当场一样。因此,如果我不能亲自去祭祀的话,我就认为我没有去祭祀。”

Confucius said: “When a person offers sacrifice to the dead, he should feel as if the dead were present. When a person offers sacrifice to the spirits, he should feel as if the spirits were present. If I could not go to the place to offer sacrifice, I would consider I did not offer sacrifice.”

子曰:“里仁为美。择不处仁,焉得知?”

孔子说:“当一个人去找地方居住时,他应当选择有仁德的人居住的地方,如果不如此,那这个人怎能还算是一个聪明人呢?”

Confucius said: “When a man chooses a place to live, he should choose a neighborhood with virtuous people. If he does not, how can he be called a wise man?”

子曰:“不仁者,不可以久处约,不可以久快乐。仁者安仁,知者利仁。”

孔子说:“没有仁德的人不能长期过贫困的生活,也不能长期过安乐的生活。只有仁德的人能享受仁德的生活,只有智慧的人能获得仁德生活的好处。”

Confucius said: “A person who is not virtuous will not live in poverty for too long. A person who is not virtuous will not live in prosperity for too long, either. Only a person of virtue is able to enjoy a virtuous life, and only a person of wisdom is able to benefit a virtuous life.”

子曰:“唯仁者能好人,能恶人。”

孔子说:“只有仁德的人才知道如何用正当的方法去喜欢一个人,或不喜欢一个人。”

Confucius said: “Only a man of virtue knows how to use the proper way to like a person or dislike a person.”

子曰:"苟志于仁矣,无恶也。"

孔子说:"如果一个人决心去做一个仁者,他就不会去做坏事的。"

Confucius said: "If a man decides to be a man of virtue, he will not do evil things."

子曰:"富与贵,是人之所欲也。不以其道得之,不处也。贫与贱,是人之所恶也,不以其道得之,不去也。君子云仁,恶乎成名?君子无终食之间违仁,造次必于是,颠沛必于是。"

孔子说:"富与贵是每一个人都想要的,如果以不正当的方法去获得,我是不会要的。贫穷和卑贱是每一个人所讨厌的,如果以不正当的方法去掉,我是不会去掉的。一个君子如果没有仁德之心,那还能算是个君子吗?一个君子终身保有仁德之心,不论是在顿饭之间,或是匆促之间,或是流离失所之时,他都是永远保有仁德之心的。"

Confucius said: "Riches and nobility are what everybody desires. But, if I used an improper way to get them, I would not keep them. Poverty and humble are what everybody wants to avoid. But, if I could not use the proper way to get rid of them, I would not do it. If a superior man abandons virtue, how can he still be called a superior man? A superior man lives with virtue throughout his life. Whether in the space of a single meal, or in a moment of haste, or in a wandering life, he always clings to virtue."

子曰:“我未见好仁者、恶不仁者。好仁者,无以尚之;恶不仁者,其为仁矣,不使不仁者加乎其身。”

孔子说:“我从没有见到过一个真正喜欢仁德或真正厌恶不仁德的人。真正喜欢仁德的人会认为仁德是至高无上无以复加的。一个不喜欢不仁德的人会不断地实行仁德而不做任何不仁德的事情。”

Confucius said: “I have never seen a person who really loved virtue, or one who really hated what was not virtuous. He who loves virtue will consider nothing above virtue. He who hates what is not virtuous will practice virtue so much that he will not do any not virtuous thing.”

子曰:“人之过也,各于其党。观过,斯知仁矣。”

孔子说:“从一个人的过错可以看出这个人的个性。因此,我们只要观察这个人的过错,就可以知道这个人是否是个仁德的人了。”

Confucius said: “People’s faults are characteristic of a person. Therefore, by observing a person’s faults, we can tell if he is a virtuous man or not.”

子曰:“朝闻道,夕死可矣。”

孔子说:“如果一个人能够明了生命的真正意义,即使他早上才明了,他也可以在晚间死去而无遗憾。”

Confucius said: “If a person understands the meaning of life, even if he just gains it in the morning, he may die in the evening without regret.”

子曰:“士志于道而耻恶衣恶食者,未足与议也。”

孔子说:“如果一个士人决心去研究生命的意义而以穿着破旧、饮食粗糙为耻的话,对于这种人我就认为不值得跟他谈论了。”

Confucius said: “If a scholar has decided to learn the meaning of life, yet he is ashamed of wearing shabby clothes and eating poor food, he will not be a worthwhile person for me to talk with.”

子曰:“君子之于天下也,无适也,无莫也,义之与比。”

孔子说:“君子对于世界上的诸事诸物是没有偏好没有成见的,他只遵从义理。”

Confucius said: “A superior man in his judgment of the world has no predilections nor prejudices; all he follows is what is right.”

子曰:“君子怀德,小人怀土。君子怀刑,小人怀惠。”

孔子:“君子只想到美德,小人只想到舒适。君子只知依法行事,小人只想到什么好处可以得到。”

Confucius said: “A superior man thinks of virtue, while an inferior man thinks of comfort. A superior man makes his choices according to justice, while an inferior man makes his choices according to what favors he will receive.”

子曰:“放于利而行,多怨。”

孔子说:“如果一个人凡事只想到可以得到什么好处,他迟早会遭到怨恨的。”

Confucius said: “If a person wants to do everything based upon advantages he will receive, sooner or later he will receive regret in return.”

子曰:“君子喻于义,小人喻于利。”

孔子说:“君子明白义理,小人只知道利益。”

Confucius said: “A superior man knows what is right, while an inferior man only knows what is advantageous to him.”

子曰:“见贤思齐焉。见不贤而内自省也。”

孔子说:“当我们遇到一个有贤德的人时我们应当想如何可以和他一样。当我们遇到一个不贤德的人时,我们应当反省如何不要像他一样。”

Confucius said: “When we see a man of virtue, we should strive to be a person like him. When we see a man of no virtue, we should strive to be not a person like him.”

子曰:“事父母几谏,见志不从,又敬不违,劳而不怨。”

孔子说:“当我们事奉父母时发现父母亲错了,应该委婉劝告。如果父母亲不听,态度仍要恭敬。即使一再发生,也不可有怨言。”

Confucius said: “When we serve our parents and find that they are wrong, we should give them advice gently. If they do not listen to us, we should still treat them with respect. Even if this happens again and again, we should not complain.”

子曰:“父母在,不远游;游必有方。”

孔子说:“父母在世,不可以去远游;如果必须去时,应该事前禀告要到哪里去。”

Confucius said:“ While parents are alive,we should not travel too far. If we have to travel,we must tell parents where we go.”

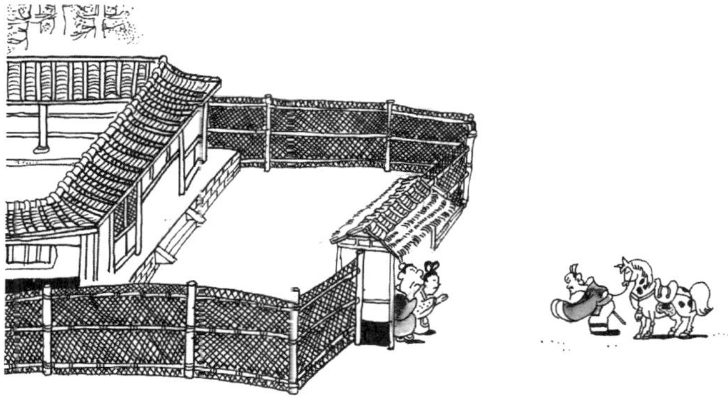

子曰:“父母之年不可不知也。一则以喜,一则以惧。”

孔子说:‘父母亲的年龄不可以不记得。如果父母享有高寿,应当欢喜;可也要担忧,因为年龄大的人来日不多。”

Confucius said: “ We should keep our parents’ ages in mind as a matter of joy, because parents live a long life, and also as a matter of fear, because old people die earlier.”

子曰:“以约失之者鲜矣。”

孔子说:“一个人做事小心,就会很少发生错误。”

Confucius said: “ A person who is careful in action will seldom make mistakes.”

子曰:“君子欲讷于言,而敏于行。”

孔子说:“君子要讲话谨慎,做事敏捷。”

Confucius said: “ A superior man speaks cautiously, and acts diligently.”

子曰:“德不孤,必有邻。”

孔子说:“有德行的人是不会孤独的,因为有很多人会愿意做他的邻居。”

Confucius said: “A person of virtue will not be lonely, for many people like to be his neighbors.”

子谓子贱:“君子哉若人!鲁无君子者,斯焉取斯?”

孔子讲到子贱,说:“这真是个君子!如果鲁国没有君子,他到哪里去取范呢?”

Confucius said of Zi Jian: “What a superior man he is! If there have never been superior men in Lu, how did he acquire his superior character?”

或曰:“雍也仁而不佞。”
子曰:“焉用佞?御人以口给,屡憎于人。
不知其仁,焉用佞?”

有人说:“雍是一个仁者,不过他没有口才。”
孔子听到后说:“我们需要口才做什么?滔滔不绝的口才只会使人厌烦。我不知道雍是否真是一个仁者,可我看不出需要口才做什么?”

Somebody said: “Yung is a man of virtue, but he does not have eloquence.”
Confucius heard this and remarked, “What do we need eloquence for? Too much eloquence could be disgusting. I don’t know If Yung is a man of virtue, but I do not see what we need eloquence for?”

子贡曰:“我不欲人之加诸我也,吾亦欲无加诸人。”
子曰: “赐也,非尔所及也。”

子贡说:“凡是我不希望别人对待我的,我也不会用来对待别人。”
孔子说:“对是对的,不过你还没有达到这个程度。”

Zi Gong said: “What I don’t want people to do to me, I won’t do it to the other people.”
Confucius said: “That is true, but you have not reached to that level yet.”

季文子三思而后行。
子闻之曰:“再,斯可矣。”

季文子凡事要思考三次才去实行。孔子听了说:“两次就够了。”

Ji Wenzi thinks three times before putting his thought into action.
When Confucius heard of this, he said: “Twice is enough.”

子曰:“宁武子,邦有道则知,邦无道则愚。其知可及也,其愚不可及也。”

孔子说:“宁武子这个人,当他的国家政治安定时,他便是一个有智慧的人;当他的国家政治不安定时,他便像是一个愚笨的人。人们容易去学他的智慧,可很难去学他的愚笨。”

Confucius said: “When order and justice prevailed in his nation, Ning Wuzi would act as a wise man. When the nation was in disorder, he acted as a stupid man. People might equal his wisdom, but it would be hard to equal his stupidity.”

子曰:“伯夷、叔齐不念旧恶,怨是用希。”

孔子说:“伯夷和叔齐不记恨别人对他们的不好,所以他们很少有怨言。”

Confucius said: “ Bo Yi and Shu Qi forgave the wrongs people made on them, so they seldom had complains.”

子曰:“孰谓微生高直?或乞醯焉,乞诸其邻而与之。”

孔子说:“谁说微生高是个诚实的人?有人向他借点醋,他没有可并不直告,而向邻家去借后交给这个人。”

Confucius said: “ Who said that Wei Shenggao was an honest man? When somebody asked for some vinegar, he did not have it but would not tell the truth. He begged his neighbor for vinegar and then gave it to the man who asked for it.”

子曰："巧言、令色、足恭，左丘明耻之，丘亦耻之。匿怨而友其人，左丘明耻之，丘亦耻之。"

孔子说："花言巧语、态度谄媚、过分谦卑，左丘明引以为耻，我也引以为耻。隐藏怨恨而故呈友善，左丘明引以为耻，我也引以为耻。"

Confucius said: " Saying flattering words, showing flattering manners, and acting too humbly, Zuo Qiuming was ashamed of those, and I am, too. Hiding resentment and appearing friendly, Zuo Qiuming was ashamed of those, and I am, too."

子曰："已矣乎，吾未见能见其过而内自讼者也。"

孔子说："算了吧，我从未见过能去找寻自己的过错而责备自己的人。"

Confucius said: " It is sad that I have never seen a person who wants to find his own faults and blame himself."

子曰:"贤哉回也!一箪食,一瓢饮,在陋巷。人不堪其忧,回也不改其乐。贤哉回也!"

孔子说:"颜回真是一个贤德的人!他饮食非常简单,住在简陋的巷子里。一般的人都忍受不了,可是颜回甘之如饴。颜回真是贤德啊!"

Confucius said: " Yan Hui is indeed a virtuous man! Living with simple meals and drinks, in a simple narrow lane, Yan Hui is still cheerful although others may not be easy to do it. Yan Hui is indeed a virtuous man!"

子曰:"质胜文则野,文胜质则史 文质彬彬,然后君子 "

孔子说:"本性的质朴盖过了外在的文采,这个人便会粗鲁。当外在的文采盖过了本性的质朴,这个人便会虚伪。只有本性的质朴和外在的文采相互协调,这个人才会是个君子。"

Confucius said: " When a man's natural qualities are in excess of his accomplishments, the man will be rude. When a man's accomplishments are in excess of his natural qualities, the man will be disguising. Only when a man's natural qualities and accomplishments are properly blended, the man will become a superior man."

子曰:“人之生也直,罔之生也幸而免。”

孔子说:“人天生是正直的。如这个人不再正直了而仍然活着,那是他的侥幸。”

Confucius said: “A man is born to be righteous. If a man loses his righteousness and still lives, it is because he is lucky.”

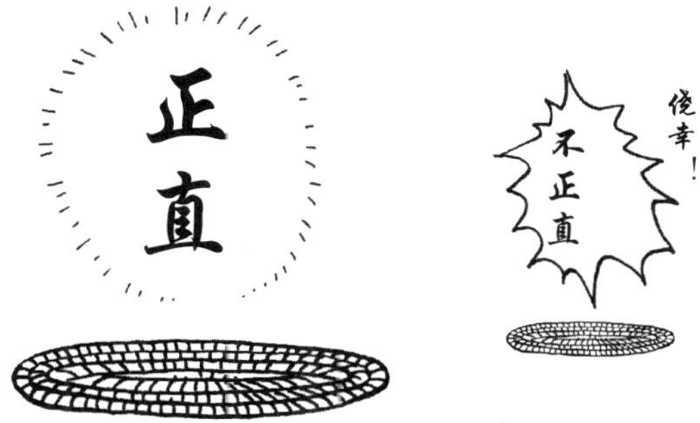

樊迟问知。
子曰:“务民之义,敬鬼神而远之,可谓知矣。”
问仁。
曰:“仁者先难而后获,可谓仁矣。”

樊迟问孔子智的定义。
孔子说:“服务民众要热诚,对于鬼和神要敬而远之,这就叫做智。”
樊迟又问仁的定义是什么。
孔子说:“有仁德的人遇到困难的事情时会率先去做,遇到有奖赏的时候会走在别人的后面,这就是仁了。”

Fan Chi asked the meaning of wisdom.
Confucius answered : “Serving the people earnestly and respecting the spiritual beings but keeping away from them is called wisdom.”
Then Fan Chi asked for the meaning of virtue. Confucius said: “A man of virtue goes ahead to take the difficult job before others, and goes behind after others when it is time to receive rewards. It's called virtue.”

子曰:"知者乐水,仁者乐山。知者动,仁者静。知者乐,仁者寿。"

孔子说:"有智慧的人喜欢流水,有仁德的人喜欢高山。有智慧的人喜欢动的境界,有仁德的人喜欢静的境界。有智慧的人享受生命的快乐,有仁德的人享有高寿。"

Confucius said: " A man of wisdom finds pleasure in the scenery of water, while a man of virtue finds pleasure in the scenery of the mountains. A man of wisdom is active while a man of virtue is tranquil. A man of wisdom enjoys life while a man of virtue lives longer."

宰我问曰:"仁者虽告之曰:'井有仁焉。'其从之也?"
子曰:"何为其然也?君子可逝也,不可陷也;可欺也,不可罔也。"

宰我问孔子:"如果告诉一个仁者在这井里也有个仁者,那他是否会到井里去找寻?"
孔子说:"他应当去吗?一个仁者可以被引进一个境界,但他不会毫不考虑地陷进去的。他可以被欺骗,但不会被愚弄。"

Zai Wo asked: "If a man of virtue was told that there was another man of virtue in the well, would he go to the well to look for?"
Confucius answered: "Should he? A man of virtue might be led to hurry to the scene, but he would not step into the scene without careful consideration. He might be imposed upon, but he would not be fooled."

子曰:“君子博学于文,约之以礼,亦可以弗畔矣夫。”

孔子说:“君子学习各种知识,遵守礼法,如此就不会做超越礼法的事。”

Confucius said: “A superior man studies all the teachings and keeps himself restrained by the rules of propriety. In doing these, he will not overstep what is proper.”

子曰:“中庸之为德也,其至矣乎。民鲜久矣。”

孔子说:“中庸是最高的仁德,可惜人们已经很久不重视它了。”

Confucius said: “Constant humility is a perfect virtue. Unfortunately, people have not practiced it for a long time.”

子曰:“仁,远乎哉?我欲仁,斯仁至矣!”

孔子说:“仁是遥远的吗?当我要达到仁的境界时,仁就在这儿!”

Confucius said: “ Is virtue a thing remote? When I want to be virtuous, virtue is here!”

子曰:“君子坦荡荡,小人长戚戚。”

孔子说:“君子往往是泰然自若的,小人是经常多虑的。”

Confucius said: “ A superior man is always composed, while an inferior man is always worrying.”

子曰:“恭而无礼则劳,慎而无礼则葸,勇而无礼则乱,直而无礼则绞。君子笃于亲,则民兴于仁。故旧不遗,则民不偷。”

孔子说:“恭敬而不守礼法是徒劳,谨慎而不守礼法是胆怯,勇敢而不守礼法是作乱,正直而不守礼法是粗鲁。当一个掌权的人去照顾他的亲人,人民就会去学他也照顾亲人走向仁道;当一个掌权的人去照顾他的朋友,人民就会去学他也照顾朋友。”

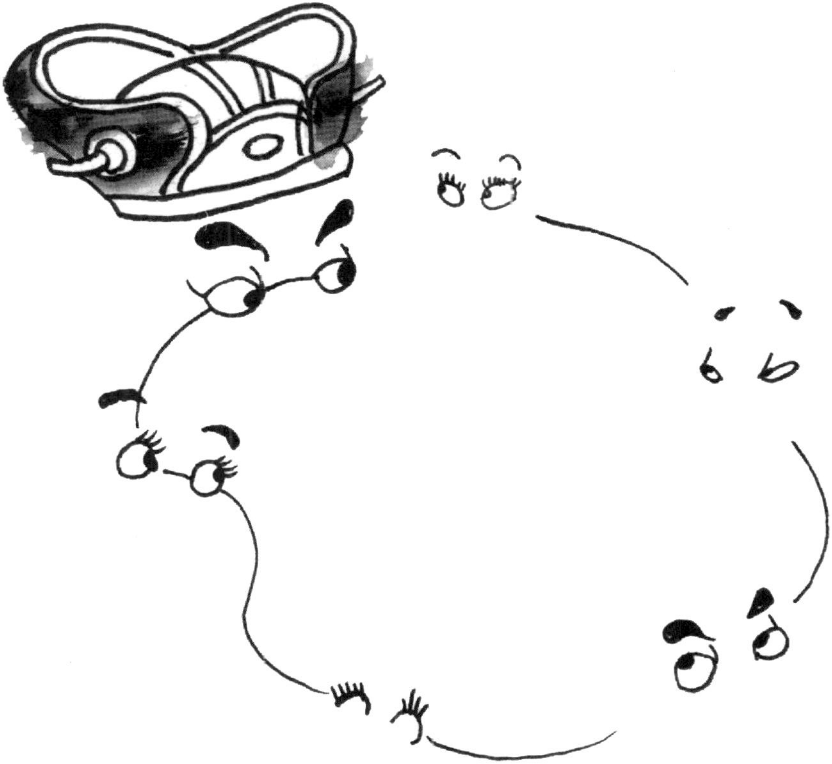

Confucius said: “Being respectful without the rules of propriety is to be laborious. Being cautious without the rules of propriety is to be timid. Being brave without the rules of propriety is to be insubordinate. Being straightforward without the rules of propriety is to be rude. When a man in power takes good care of his families and relatives, the people will learn from him and take good care of their families and relatives, and everybody will work toward virtue. When a man in power takes care of his old friends, the people will follow this example and do the same.”

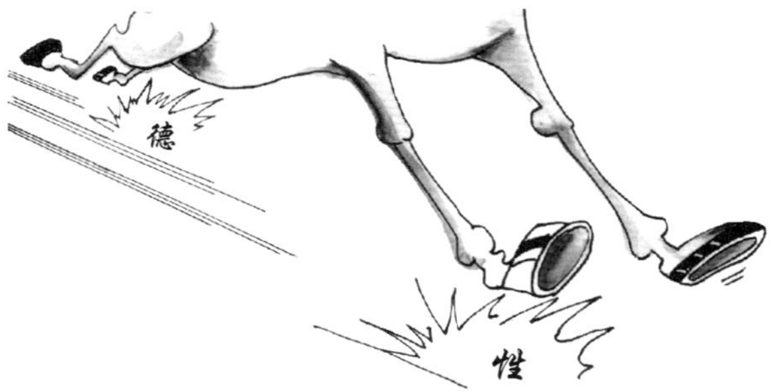


曾子曰:“士,不可以不弘毅。任重而道远,仁以为己任,不亦重乎?死而后已,不亦远乎?”

曾子说:“一个受过教育的正直的人,不可以没有弘大坚毅的德性。他的责任是重大而且长远的,以达到仁的境界作为他的责任,这不是一个重大的责任么?要终身从事此一任务,那不是很长远的么?”

Zeng Zi said: “An educated gentleman may not be without resoluteness in his character. His responsibility is heavy and long. His responsibility is to carry out virtue. Is this a heavy responsibility? To carry out his responsibility until he dies. Is this a long responsibility?”

子曰:“学如不及,犹恐失之。”

孔子说:“一个人应当不断去学习就好像从来没有达到目的似的,而且还要害怕那已经学到的会遗忘。”

Confucius said: “A man should keep learning as if he has never reached his target. Meanwhile, he should be afraid of losing what he has learned.”

子曰:“知者不惑,仁者不忧,勇者不惧。”

孔子说:“有智慧的人是不会迷惑的,有仁德的人是不会忧郁的,有勇气的人是不会惧怕的。”

Confucius said: “A man of wisdom is free from perplexities; a man of virtue is free from anxiety; and a man of courage is free from fear.”

颜渊问仁。
子曰:“克己复礼为仁。一日克己复礼,天下归仁焉。为仁由己,而由人乎哉!”
颜渊曰:“请问其目。”
子曰:“非礼勿视,非礼勿听,非礼勿言,非礼勿动。”
颜渊曰:“回虽不敏,请事斯语矣。”

颜渊问孔子仁的定义。
孔子说:“控制自己同时做事要符合礼仪就是仁。一旦这个人能做到了,天下的人都会说他是个仁者。所以达到仁的境界与否是由他自己来决定的,岂是由别人处得来的吗!”
颜渊说:“请说得详细一点。”
孔子说:“违背礼仪的东西不要去看,违背礼仪的东西不要去听,违背礼仪的话语不要去说,违背礼仪事情不要去做。”
颜渊说:“虽然我不是聪明人,我将照着去做。”

Yan Yuan asked about the perfect virtue.
Confucius said: “Controlling oneself and doing everything according to the rules of propriety is perfect virtue. Once a man can do these, people in the world will all say he is a man of virtue. Therefore, the practice of virtue comes from within the man himself, not from others.”
Yan Yuan then asked for details.
Confucius said: “Don’t look at what is contrary to propriety; don’t listen to what is contrary to propriety; don’t speak what is contrary to propriety; and don’t do what is contrary to propriety.”
Yan Yuan said: “Although I am not smart, I am going to practice this lesson.”

仲弓问仁。
子曰:“出门如见大宾,使民如承大祭。己所不欲,勿施于人。在邦无怨,在家无怨。”
仲弓曰:“雍虽不敏,请事斯语矣。”

仲弓问孔子仁的定义。
孔子说:“出门的时候,就好像要去会见贵重的宾客;役使民众的时候,就好像要去参加一个重大的祭祀。凡是你不喜欢别人对待你的,你也不要那样去对待别人。不论你在邦国里还是在家里,都没有人怨恨你。”
仲弓说:“虽然我不是聪明人,我将照着去做。”

Zhong Gong asked about the perfect virtue.
Confucius said: “Whenever you leave your home, you must behave toward everybody as if you were visiting an important guest. Whenever you need to employ people, you must be very sincere as if you were attending a great sacrifice. Do not treat others in a way which you would not like others to treat you. Give no cause for complaint in the nation as well as at home.”
Zhong Gong said: “Although I am not smart, I am going to practice this lesson.”

司马牛问仁。
子曰:“仁者其言也讱。”
曰:“其言也讱斯谓之仁矣乎?”
子曰:“为之难,言之得无讱乎?”

司马牛问孔子仁的定义。
孔子说:“仁者讲话很小心谨慎。”
司马牛问:“讲话小心谨慎就算是仁吗?”
孔子说:“当一个人感觉到做好一件事情很难时,他说话的时候能不小心谨慎吗?”

Si Maniu asked about the perfect virtue.
Confucius said: “A man of virtue speaks slowly and cautiously.”
Si Maniu asked: “Speaking slowly and cautiously can mean virtue?”
Confucius said: “When a man feels that it is difficult to accomplish a mission, can he not help but speak slowly and cautiously?”

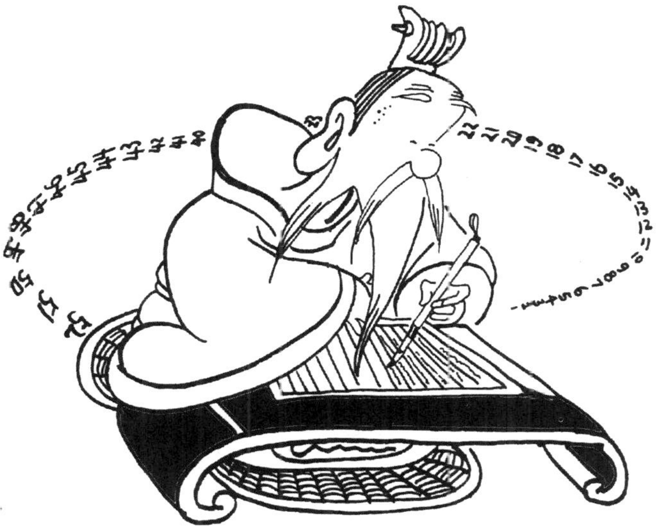

司马牛问君子。
子曰:“君子不忧不惧。”
曰:“不忧不惧斯谓之君子已乎?”
子曰:“内省不疚,夫何忧何惧?”

司马牛问孔子君子的定义。
孔子说:“君子是不忧愁和不畏惧的。”
司马牛问:“不忧愁和不畏惧就是君子吗?”
孔子说:“当一个人反省一生中没有做过错事时,哪还有忧愁和畏惧呢?”

Si Maniu asked what a superior man is.
Confucius said: “A superior man has neither worry nor fear.”
Si Maniu asked: “Having no worry or fear means a superior man?”
Confucius said: “When a man examines his life and finds nothing wrong he has done, what will he have worry and fear for?”

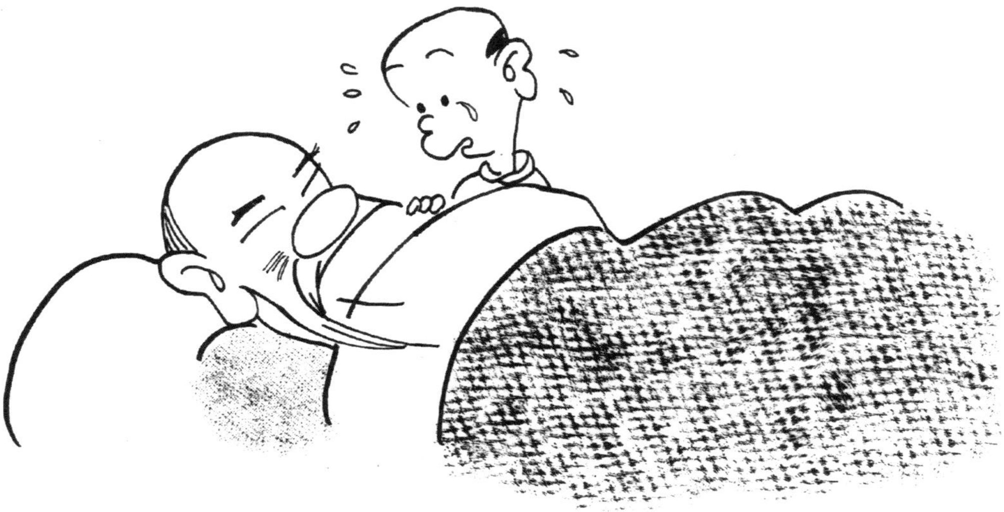

司马牛忧曰:“人皆有兄弟，我独亡。”

子夏曰:“商闻之矣,‘死生有命,富贵在天。’君子敬而无失,与人恭而有礼,四海之内皆兄弟也。君子何患乎无兄弟也?”

司马牛埋怨说:“别人都有兄弟,可是我没有。”

子夏安慰他说:“我听说过:‘一个人的生和死是由命运决定的,富和贵是老天安排的。’一个君子只要做事谨慎无误,对待别人恭谦有礼貌,那全世界的人都会做你的兄弟的。为什么一个君子还要忧虑没有兄弟呢?”

Si Maniu complained about having no brothers.

Zi Xia comforted him: “I have heard, ‘A person’s life and death depend upon his fate . Riches and honors are arranged by the Heaven.’ When a superior man does things cautiously, without faults, treating people humbly and respectfully, all the people in the world are willing to be his brothers.So why should a superior man worry about having no brothers?”

子张问明。
子曰:“浸润之谮,肤受之愬,不行焉,可谓明也已矣。浸润之谮 肤受之愬,不行焉,可谓远也已矣。”

子张问孔子明的定义。
孔子说:“一个人如能不受直接及间接的诽谤所伤害,这个人便是明智之人。一个人如能不受直接及间接的诽谤所伤害,他可以说是个有远见的人。”

Zi Zhang asked about intelligence.
Confucius said: “The person who can resist slander directly and indirectly without being hurt may be called a person of intelligence. The person who can resist slander directly and indirectly without being hurt may be called a person of far-sight.”

子张问崇德辨惑。
子曰:"主忠信,徙义,崇德也。爱之欲其生,恶之欲其死,既欲其生,又欲其死,是惑也。"

子张问孔子如何增强德性辨别困惑。
孔子说:"对人忠诚信实,做合乎义理的事情,你的德性便会增强了。喜爱一个人就要这个人生活得好,不喜爱一个人就要这个人早点死亡,既要他生活得好,又要他早死,就是困惑。"

Zi Zhang asked how to improve virtue and how to dispel delusions in life.
Confucius said: " Be faithful and sincere to everyone, and do only whatever is right; then your virtue will improve. When a person loves another person, he wants the person he loves to live very well. When a person hates another person, he wants the person he hates to die early. Sometime, a person loves and hates a person at the same time. He wants the person to live very well; meanwhile, he also wants the person to die early. That is called a delusion."

子曰:“君子成人之美,不成人之恶。小人反是。”

孔子说:“一个君子喜欢帮助别人完成好的事情,不喜欢帮助别人完成坏的事情。小人则是完全相反。”

Confucius said: “A superior man likes to help others finish a good deed, but he will not help others finish a bad deed. An inferior man does the opposite.”

樊迟问仁。
子曰:“居处恭,执事敬,与人忠,虽之夷狄,不可弃也。”

樊迟问孔子仁的定义。
孔子说:“与家人相处,必须真诚,做事必须慎重。与人相处,应该忠实。不管住在哪儿,就是住在蛮夷之处,都不可忽略这些原则。”

Fan Chi asked about the perfect virtue.
Confucius said: “At home, a person must be sincere. In business, he must be serious. In dealing with people, he must be faithful. No matter where he lives, even in an uncivilized place, he should never neglect these principles.”

子曰:“君子和而不同,小人同而不和。”

孔子说:“君子与人和蔼相处,但不同流合污;小人同流合污,但不能与人和蔼相处。”

Confucius said: “A superior man is affable to people, but does not go with the stream, while an inferior man goes with the stream, but is not affable.”

子曰:“君子泰而不骄,小人骄而不泰。”

孔子说:“君子坦荡舒泰,而不骄傲;小人骄傲,而不坦荡舒泰。”

Confucius said: “A superior man is composed, but not proud; an inferior man is proud, but not composed.”

子曰:“刚、毅、木、讷,近仁。”

孔子说:“刚正、坚毅、质朴和讷言的德性接近仁。”

Confucius said: “The firm, resolute, simple, and modest character is closely approaching virtue.”

子路问曰:“何如斯可谓之士矣?”
子曰:“切切偲偲,怡怡如也,可谓士矣。朋友切切偲偲,兄弟怡怡。”

子路问孔子:“如何才可以叫做士人?”
孔子说:“士人互相勉励切磋,和气亲切。朋友之间互相勉励切磋;兄弟之间,和气亲切。”

Zi Lu asked: “What qualities must a man possess in order to be called a scholar?”
Confucius said: “Scholars study together and encourage each other, and scholars are pleasant and affectionate. Toward friends, they study together and encourage each other. Toward brothers, they are pleasant and affectionate.”

宪问耻。
子曰:“邦有道,穀。邦无道,穀,耻也。”
“克、伐、怨、欲不行焉,可以为仁矣?”
子曰:“可以为难矣,仁则吾不知也。”

宪问孔子耻的定义。
孔子说:“政治清明时,你可以做官领取俸禄。政治不清明时,你也做官领取俸禄,那就是可耻。”
宪又问:“如果一个人不争辩、不自夸、不怨艾、也不贪得,这个人可否称为仁者?”
孔子说:“这种人也可以说是难能可贵的了,至于他是否可以称为仁者,我就不知道了。”

Xian asked the meaning of shame.
Confucius said: “If the top officials governed the nation with justice, you could work for the government and receive a salary. If the top officials governed the nation without justice, but you still worked for the government because of salary, that would be a shame.”
Xian then asked: “If a man did not compete, boast, or complain, and was not greedy, could he be called a man of virtue?”
Confucius said: “There are not many such men indeed. As for if he can be called a man of virtue, I don't know.”

子曰:“士而怀居,不足以为士矣。”

孔子说:“如果一个士只想到舒适的生活,他将不配称为士。”

Confucius said: “If a scholar only thinks of the comforts of life, he should not be called a scholar.”

子曰:“邦有道,危言危行;邦无道,危行言孙。”

孔子说:“政治清明时,你可以作正直的言行;政治不清明时,你的行为仍要正直,可是说话就要谨慎了。”

Confucius said: “With justice and order in the government, a person's speech and action must be just. Without justice and order in the government, a person's action may still be just, but when he speaks, he must be cautious.”

子曰:“有德者必有言,有言者不必有德。仁者必有勇,勇者不必有仁。”

孔子说:“仁德的人常说仁德的话语。可是,说仁德话语的人不一定都是仁德之人。仁者都是勇敢的人。可是,勇敢的人不一定都是仁者。”

Confucius said: “A virtuous man always speaks virtuous words; however, a man who speaks virtuous words is not always a virtuous man. A virtuous man always has courage; however, a courageous man is not always a virtuous man.”

子曰:“其言之不怍,则为之也难。”

孔子说:“如果一个人说话不谦逊,我们如何能盼望他会有好的行为?”

Confucius said: “If a person speaks without modesty, how can we expect much from his actions?”

子曰:"君子上达,小人下达。"

孔子说:"君子逐日上进,小人每况愈下。"

Confucius said: "A superior man makes progress daily, while an inferior man's situation makes worse daily."

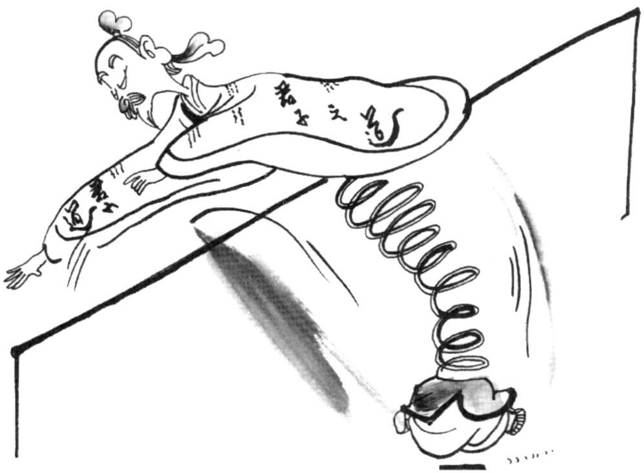

曾子曰:"君子思不出其位。"

曾子说:"君子考虑一件事情时,是不会超越他的身份地位的。"

Zeng Zi said: "When a superior man thinks of doing something, he would not think of doing the thing which is not suitable for his position."

子曰:"君子耻其言之过其行也。"

孔子说:"君子认为,如果他说了而没有做到就是耻辱。"

Confucius said: "A superior man feels shameful if he said something, he did not do it accordingly."

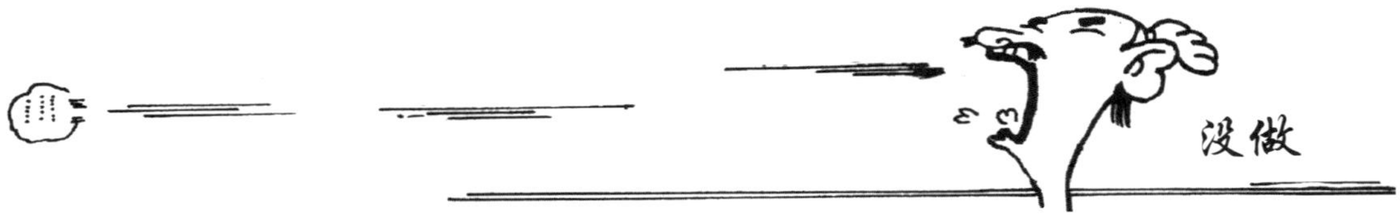

子曰:"君子道者三,我无能焉。仁者不忧,知者不惑,勇者不惧。"
子贡曰:"夫子自道也。"

孔子说:"作为一个君子应有三个要素,可我不合格。仁者是不忧虑的,有智慧的人是不会困惑的,勇敢的人是不惧怕的。"
子贡说:"这是老师在自己说自己。"

Confucius said: "A superior man
Has three qualifications which I do not have: A man of virtue is free from anxiety; a man of wisdom is free from perplexities; and a man of courage is free from fear."
Zi Gong said: "That is what our master says of himself."

子曰:“不患人之不己知,患其不能也。”

孔子说:“不要担心别人不知道你,你要担心你没有才能。”

Confucius said: “Do not be afraid of having no one know you. Be afraid of having no talent.”

或曰:“以德报怨,何如?”
子曰:“何以报德?以直报怨,以德报德。”

有人问孔子:“可以以仁德去回报怨恨吗?”
孔子说:“如果这样,那我们如何去回报仁德呢?应该以正直去处理怨恨,以仁德去回报仁德。”

Someone asked Confucius can hatred be repaid with favor?
Confucius said: “In that case, how can we repay the favor? We should handle the hatred with justice, and repay the favor with favor.”

子路问君子。
子曰："修己以敬。"
曰："如斯而已乎?"
曰："修己以安人。"
曰："如斯而矣乎?"
曰："修己以安百姓，尧舜其犹病诸。"

子路问孔子君子的定义。
孔子说："一个君子必须增进自己的品德。"
子路问："就这么样简单吗?"
孔子说："增进自己的品德可以安定其他的人。"
子路问："就这么样简单吗?"
孔子说："增进自己的品德来安定百姓，以前的尧和舜都还没有完全如此做到呢。"

Zi Lu asked what was meant by superior man.
Confucius said: "A superior man must cultivate himself."
Zi Lu then asked: "Is that all?"
Confucius said: "By cultivating himself, he can make other people peaceful."
Zi Lu asked again: "And is that all?"
Confucius said: "By cultivating himself, he can make all his people peaceful. Even the ancient emperors, Yao and Shun, could not do that."

子曰："可与言而不与言，失人。不可与言而与之言，失言。知者不失人，亦不失言。"

孔子说："当你遇到一个你应该和他讲话的人而你不讲，那就是你失掉了认识一个人的机会。当你遇到一个人你不应该与他说话而你说了，那就是你说了不应该说的话。有智慧的人是既不失掉认识人的机会，也不说不应该说的话。"

Confucius said: " When you met a person you should speak to, but you did not speak to him, you lost an opportunity to know a person.When you met a person you should not speak to, but you spoke to him anyway, you said something which you should not have spoken. A man of wisdom never loses an opportunity to know a person, nor says something which he should not speak."

子曰："志士仁人，无求生以害仁，有杀生以成仁。"

孔子说："志士和仁人不会为了保全他们的性命而去损害仁德的，只会牺牲性命而去保全仁德的。"

Confucius said: " Both a scholar of determination and a man of virtue never try to save their own lives at the expense of virtue. They are willing to give up their lives in order to preserve virtue."

子贡问为仁。
子曰:"工欲善其事,必先利其器。居是邦也,事其大夫之贤者,友其士之仁者。"

子贡问孔子做到仁的方法。
孔子说:"当一个工人要做好他的工作,就必须将他的工具修得锋利。住在一个国家,就要跟随贤明的官吏工作,与那些有仁德的士人做朋友。"

Zi Gong asked about how to practice virtue. Confucius said: "When a workman wants to do his job well, he must sharpen his tools first. Living in a nation, you should work under officials of virtue, and make friends with educated men of virtue."

子曰:"君子义以为质,礼以行之,孙以出之,信以成之。君子哉!"

孔子说:"如能做事正直,一切都按礼仪,说话谦逊,答应的都做到,这个人就是个君子!"

Confucius said: " If a man can be righteous in his actions, perform everything according to the rules of propriety, speak with humility, and carry out the things he has promised, such a man is a superior man!"

子曰:"君子病无能焉,不病人之不己知也。"

孔子说:"君子只怕没有才能,不怕别人不知道他。"

Confucius said: "A superior man is afraid of lacking ability. He is not afraid of nobody knowing him."

子曰:"君子疾没世而名不称焉。"

孔子说:"君子最恨死后没留好名声。"

Confucius said: "A superior man hates to pass away without leaving a good reputation."

子曰:“君子求诸己,小人求诸人。”

孔子说:“当麻烦发生了,君子会先责备自己,可小人就会去责怪别人。”

Confucius said: “When a problem happens, a superior man blames himself first, but an inferior man blames others.”

子曰:“君子矜而不争,群而不党。”

孔子说:“君子有尊严但不与人争论,合群但不结私党。”

Confucius said: “A superior man is dignified, but does not dispute. He is sociable, but does not party.”

子曰:"君子不以言举人,不以人废言。"

孔子说:"君子不因为某一个人说了句好话就去推荐他,但也不因为一个人的行为不端就弃绝他的任何话语。"

Confucius said: " A superior man does not recommend a person simply because he says nice words. Furthermore, he does not discard a person's words simply because that person's conduct is bad."

子贡问曰:"有一言而可以终身行之者乎?"
子曰:"其恕乎。己所不欲,勿施于人。"

子贡问孔子:"可有一言可以终身奉行吗?"
孔子说:"那就是恕字了。自己所不喜欢的,不要去施与别人。"

Zi Gong asked his master, " Is there one word which we may follow as a life rule?"
Confucius said: " The word is MERCY. It means that whatever you do not want to be done to you, do not do it to others."

子曰:“过而不改,是谓过矣。”

孔子说:“有过错而不去改,那就是真正的过错。”

Confucius said: “The worse fault is that a man does not want to correct his fault.”

子曰:“吾尝终日不食,终夜不寝,以思,无益,不如学也。”

孔子说:“我曾经整天不吃饭不睡觉去苦思,可是没有用,还是不如去学习的好。”

Confucius said: “ To improve my thinking, I did not eat for a whole day and did not sleep for a whole night.It did not work. Now I would rather study.”

子曰:“知及之,仁不能守之,虽得之,必失之。知及之,仁能守之,不庄以莅之,则民不敬。知及之,仁能守之,庄以莅之,动之不以礼,未善也。”

孔子说:“聪明才智足以得到它,惟如德行不能守住它,虽然已经得到它,仍会失去的。聪明才智足以得到它,德行也能守住它,如果不能庄严地站在职位上,老百姓是不会敬服的。聪明才智足以得到它,德行也能守住它,并能庄严地站在职位上,惟如做事不按礼法,那还不能算是完美的。”

Confucius said: “With his wisdom, when a man attains a knowledge, if he does not have the virtue to hold it, whatever he has attained will be lost. When a man attains a knowledge and he also has the virtue to hold onto it, if he can not keep his position with dignity, people will not respect nor believe him. When he attains knowledge, has the virtue to hold onto it, and keeps his position with dignity, if his actions are not right according to the rules of propriety, he is still not perfect.”

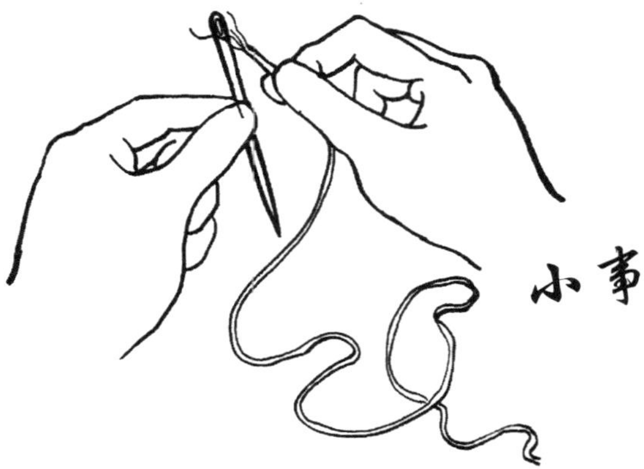


子曰:"君子不可小知,而可大受也。小人不可大受,而可小知也。"

孔子说:"君子有时小事情做不好,可是大事情能够做好。小人大事情做不好,可是有时小事情可以做好。"

Confucius said:" A superior man sometimes can not do small things very well, but he can accomplish big missions. An inferior man can not accomplish big missions, but sometimes he can do small things very well."

子曰:"民之于仁也,甚于水火。水火吾见蹈而死者矣,未见蹈仁而死者也。"

孔子说:"仁德之对于人民比水火还要重要。我曾经看过有人死于水火之灾的,可我从未见过有人死于仁德的。"

Confucius said: " In life, virtue is more important than water or fire. I have seen people die from falling into water or fire, but I have never seen people die from falling into virtue."

子曰:“当仁不让于师。”

孔子说:“在仁德的大道理上,连对老师也不谦让的。”

Confucius said: “When virtue is needed, a man should not yield, not even to his teacher.”

子曰:“君子贞而不谅。”

孔子说:“君子做事根据正大的原则,他是不必要去遵守小节的。”

Confucius said: “A superior man does things according to the main principles. He does not have to stick to small promises.”

子曰:“君子有三戒:少之时,血气未定,戒之在色;及其壮也,血气方刚,戒之在斗;及其老也,血气既衰,戒之在得。”

孔子说:“君子有三个警戒:少年时,血气尚未成形,必须节制情欲。长大后,血气正在旺盛,必须节制与人打斗。到了老年的时候,血气已经衰退,必须节制贪得无厌。”

Confucius said: “A man should beware of three things. In youth, when the constitution of his body is not completely formed, he should beware of lust. In manhood, when the constitution of his body is completely formed and in full vigor, he should beware of strife. In old age, when his physical condition is in decay, he should beware of greed.”

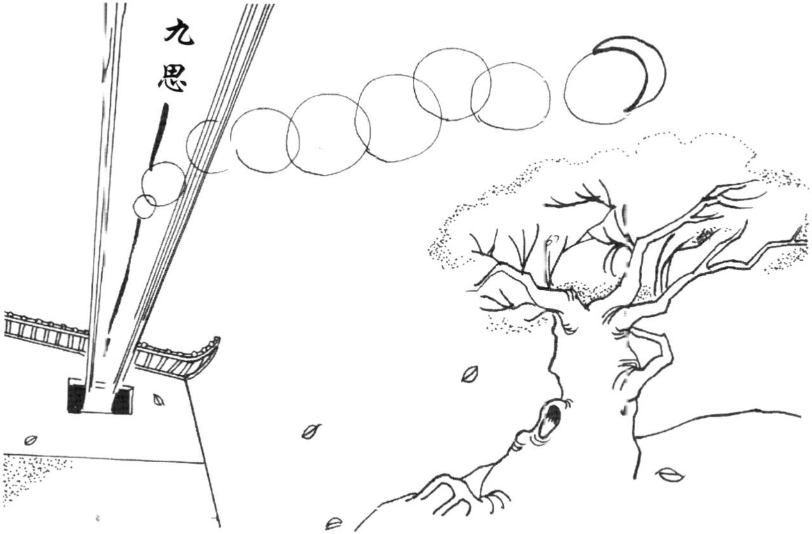


孔子曰:"君子有九思:视思明,听思聪,色思温,貌思恭,言思忠,事思敬,疑思问,忿思难,见得思义。"

孔子说:"君子有九个希望:(1) 当他看东西时,他希望能看得清楚。(2) 当他听时,他希望能听得清楚。(3) 他希望他的面貌看起来很温和。(4) 他希望他的态度很谦逊。(5) 当他说话时,他希望他说的话是诚恳的。(6) 当他做事时,他希望他是认真的。(7) 当他有怀疑时,他希望他能问个明白。(8) 当他发怒时,他希望能想到后果的严重。(9) 当他见到要有利益时,他希望能想想这是否是他应该得到的。"

Confucius said: "A superior man has nine 'wants': (1) When he sees something, he wants to see it clearly. (2) When he hears something, he wants to hear it distinctly. (3) In his facial expression, he wants to look kind. (4) In his manner, he wants to be humble. (5) When he speaks, he wants to be honest. (6) When he does things, he wants to be serious. (7) When he has doubt he wants to ask. (8) When he is angry, he wants to think of consequences. (9) When he is about to have a personal advantage, he wants to think whether he should take it or not."

子张问仁于孔子。
孔子曰:“能行五者于天下为仁矣。”
“请问之。”
曰:“恭、宽、信、敏、惠。恭则不侮,宽则得众,信则人任焉,敏则有功,惠则足以使人。”

子张问孔子仁的定义。
孔子说:“不论这个人走到哪儿都能做到这五点就是仁了。”
子张问:“哪五点?”
孔子说:“恭敬、宽容、信赖、勤奋、惠爱。对人恭敬不会受到侮辱。宽容容易赢得友谊。一个值得信赖的人会受到人们的信任。勤奋可以成就很多事情。惠爱会使人们愿意为他效劳。”

Zi Zhang asked Confucius about the perfect virtue.
Confucius said: “Perfect virtue is being able to carry out five things wherever one goes.”
Zi Zhang asked: “Which five?”
Confucius replied: “Respect, forgiveness, trustworthiness, diligence, and generosity. When he is respectful, he will not be insulted. When he is forgiving, he will win friendship. When he is trustworthy, he can be relied upon by others. When he is diligent, he will accomplish much. When he is generous, he will find people willing to serve him.”

子曰:“由也,女闻六言六蔽矣乎?”
对曰:“未也。”
“居,吾语女。好仁不好学,其蔽也愚。好知不好学,其蔽也荡。好信不好学,其蔽也贼。好直不好学,其蔽也绞。好勇不好学,其蔽也乱。好刚不好学,其蔽也狂。”

孔子问他的学生:“由啊,你可听到过六种美德及六种弊病吗?”
由说:“没有。”
孔子说:“你坐下,让我来告诉你。喜好仁德但不喜欢学习,是愚昧。喜好知识但不喜欢学习,是放荡。喜好诚信但不喜欢学习,是损害。喜好正直但不喜欢学习,是急躁。喜好勇敢但不喜欢学习,是作乱。喜好刚强但不喜欢学习,是狂妄。”

Confucius said to his disciple: “ You, have you heard of six kinds of virtues and their failure?”
You said: “Not yet.”
Confucius said: “ Sit down. Let me tell you. Wanting to be benevolent without learning will lead to stupidity. Wanting to have knowledge without learning will lead to dissipation. Wanting to be sincere without learning will lead to injury. Wanting to be just without learning will lead to haste. Wanting to be bold without learning will lead to insubordination. Wanting to be firm without learning will lead to extravagance.”

子路曰:"君子尚勇乎?"
子曰:"君子义以为上。君子有勇而无义,为乱。小人有勇而无义,为盗。"

子路问孔子:"君子也崇尚勇猛吗?"孔子说:"君子认为义理是最高的原则。如果君子认为勇猛最重要,他将为国家带来混乱。如果小人崇尚勇猛,他将成为盗贼。"

Zi Lu asked: " Does a superior man consider bravery to be the most important quality?"
Confucius said: " The superior man holds righteousness to be the most important quality. If a superior man considered bravery the most important, he would cause great chaos in the nation. If an inferior man considered bravery the most important, he would likely become a robber."

子贡曰:“君子亦有恶乎?”
子曰:“有恶。恶称人之恶者。恶居下流而讪上者。恶勇而无礼者。恶果敢而窒者。”
曰:“赐也,亦有恶乎?”
“恶徼以为知者。恶不孙以为勇者。恶讦以为直者。”

子贡问孔子:“君子也有厌恶吗?”
孔子说:“君子有厌恶。他厌恶那些喜欢宣扬别人短处的人。他厌恶那些居于下位却喜欢诽谤在他上位的人。他厌恶那些勇猛但不遵守礼仪的人。他厌恶那些有决断但不通事理的人。”
接着孔子问子贡:“你也有厌恶吗?”
子贡说:“我厌恶那些袭取别人的意见而自认为是聪明的人。我厌恶那些不谦逊而自认为是勇敢的人。我厌恶那些喜欢传播别人的隐私而自认为是正直的人。”

Zi Gong asked: “Does a superior man have any dislikes?”
Confucius said: “Yes, a superior man has dislikes. He dislikes the people who elaborate upon other people’s weaknesses. He dislikes the people in lower positions detract the people in higher positions. He dislikes the people who are brave but do not observe the rules of propriety. He dislikes the people who show determination, but unreasonable.”
Then, Confucius asked Zi Gong if he also had any dislikes.
Zi Gong said: “I dislike people who steal other people’s discovery, but think they are smart. I dislike people who are not modest, but think they are brave. I dislike people who reveal other person’s secrets, but declare they are fair.”

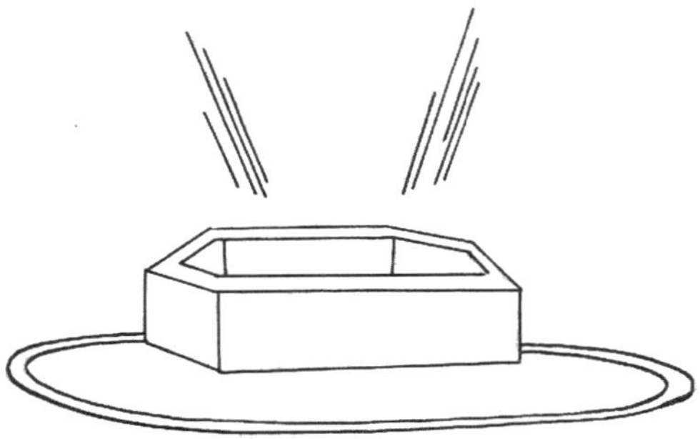

子张曰:"士,见危致命,见得思义,祭思敬,丧思哀,其可已矣。"

子张说:"当一个人遇到了危险时,只要他认为是对的,就是有性命之忧他也不顾。当他见到了将有机会得到什么利益时,他会首先考虑是否应该获得然后去拿。当他在祭祀时,他的态度是虔诚的。当他参加丧礼时,他表达了哀伤。如果一个人能做到这些,那他可以称为一个士人。"

Zi Zhang said: "When a man faces danger, he is not afraid of giving up his life if he thinks what he is doing is right. When he sees an opportunity to gain, he will think first whether the gain is righteous before he takes it. When he is in worship, he is devout and sincere. When he attends a funeral, he shows his heartfelt grief. If a person can do all of these, he will surely be called a scholar."

子张曰:"执德不弘,信道不笃,焉能为有?焉能为亡?"

子张说:"虽说有仁德,可缺少决心去增强;相信正道,但又不坚定,这样的人怎能称为有德之人?"

Zi Zhang said: "Having virtue, but lacking determination to increase it; believing the right principles, but lacking sincerity; how could such a man be called a man of virtue?"

子夏曰:“博学而笃志,切问而近思,仁在其中矣。”

子夏说:“当一个人努力去博学,志向又坚定,急切探讨,自我反省,他便可以获得仁德了。”

Zi Xia said: “When a man tries to learn extensively, and his goal is firm, inquires with earnestness, and reflects with self-application, his virtue is on the right course.”

子夏曰:“大德不逾闲,小德出入可也。”

子夏说:“如能在大节的地方完全遵守,小节上面是可以不太计较的。”

Zi Xia said: “If a man strictly adheres to the major points of virtue, he may use his discretion to handle the small points of virtue.”

# 第二章
# CHAPTER TWO

## 如何从政
## HOW TO BE IN POLITICS

子曰:"道千乘之国,敬事而信,节用而爱人,使民以时。"

孔子说:"管理一个有千辆战车的大国必须有诚信,使用国家财产要有节制,对人民要有爱心,如需要人民做事时,必须选择人民有空闲的时候。"

Confucius said: "When a ruler rules a large nation, he must be honest and faithful. He must be thrifty in the utilization of expenses and must care for the people's welfare. When he must draft people to do something, he should choose the proper time when people are able."

有子曰:"礼之用,和为贵。先王之道斯为美,小大由之。有所不行,知和而和,不以礼节之,亦不可行也。"

有子说:"在礼节的施行中,和气最为重要了。古代帝王的施政中以和气最为后人所称道,无论大事小事均以和字解决。但有时也有解决不了的地方,那就是只用和气而不以礼节去节制,仍是行不通的。"

You Zi said: " In practicing the rules of propriety, harmony is the most important. The early kings emphasized the importance of harmony. All things, great or small, went with harmony. However, sometimes, if they tried to use harmony only, it would not work, because they lacked propriety to restrict it."

子曰:“为政以德,譬如北辰,居其所而众星共之。”

孔子说:“国君以仁德治国,就好像北极星高挂天空由其他众星拱卫一般。”

Confucius said: “A ruler who governs the people by means of virtue is like the polestar which keeps its place while all the other stars turn towards it.”

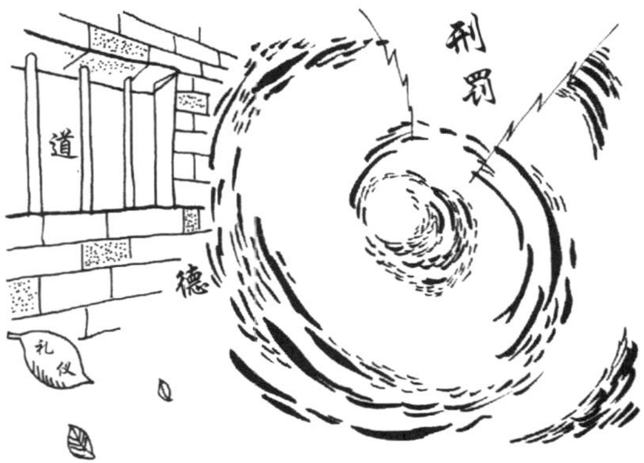


子曰:“道之以政,齐之以刑,民免而无耻。道之以德,齐之以礼,有耻且格。”

孔子说:“治理人民以法制政令,如不服从,就受刑罚,人民只知道如何避免受刑,而没有羞耻的观念。如果以道德礼仪来治理人民,人民就会知道做坏事是羞耻而不再去犯了。”

Confucius said: “When the people are governed by the laws and punished according to the laws, the wrong-doers receive the punishment. Afterwards, they only try not to receive the punishment again, but do not feel that their crimes were a shame. If the people are governed by morality and corrected by the ways of propriety, the wrong-doers will realize what they did were a shame and will not commit crime again.”

哀公问曰:“何为则民服?”
孔子对曰:“举直错诸枉,则民服。举枉错诸直,则民不服。”

哀公问孔子:“如何使人民信服?”
孔子回答:“如果你举月正直的人士担任政府的官吏,弃绝那些不正直的官吏,人民就会信服。如果你举用不正直的人做官吏,弃绝正直的人,人民就不会信服了。”

Ai, the reigning prince of Confucius' native state, Lu, asked Confucius: "How could I make the people submissive?"
Confucius replied: " If you advance the upright as officials and set aside the crooked ones, the people will submit. If you advance the crooked as officials and set aside the upright ones, the people will not submit."

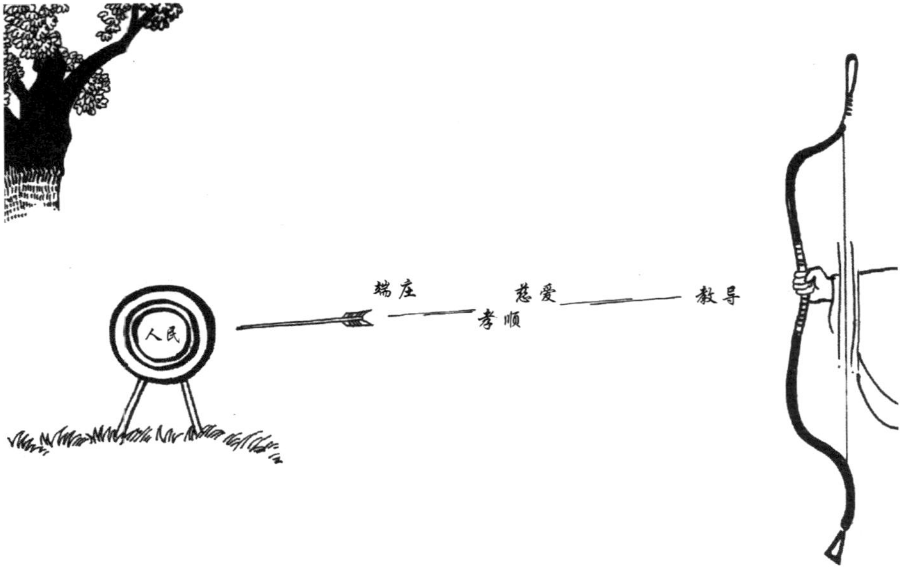


季康子问:“使民敬忠以劝,如之何?”
子曰:“临之以庄,则敬;孝慈,则忠;举善而教不能,则劝。”

季康子问:“要使人民敬仰、忠诚,及互相劝勉,如何才可以办到?”
孔子说:“接近人民时要端庄,人民就会敬仰。统治者本身要孝顺父母、慈爱年幼,人民就会忠诚。举用善良的人,教导不善良的人,人民就会互相劝勉。”

Ji Kangzi, a noble in Confucius' native state, Lu, asked Confucius: “How could I make people reverent, faithful, and willing to exert themselves with each others?”
Confucius replied: “If you approach people, your manner must be serious; then, people will be reverent. If you treat your parents with filial obedience, and treat your juniors with compassion, people will be faithful. If you advance the excellent and educate the ignorant, the people will exert themselves with each others.”

或谓孔子曰:“子奚不为政？”
子曰:“《书》云:‘孝于惟孝,友于兄弟。’施于有政,是亦为政,奚其为为政?”

有人问孔子:“你为何不从事政治?”
孔子说:“《书经》上不是说了吗:‘要孝顺父母,友爱兄弟。’把这种爱延伸到政府官吏身上去,这也叫做从事政治。为什么还要直接去从政呢？”

Some one asked Confucius: “Why don’t you take part in the government affairs?”
Confucius said: “*The Book of Records* states, ‘Treat parents with filial obedience. Treat brothers with compassion.’ Expanding the principles to the rulers means to take part in the government affairs, too. Why do I need to take part directly?”

子张问:“十世可知也?”
子曰:“殷因于夏礼,所损益可知也。周因于殷礼,所损益可知也。其或继周者,虽百世,可知也。”

子张问:“从今以后十个朝代的事情可否预知?”
孔子说:“殷代因袭夏代的礼仪,其增减多少是可以知道的。周代因袭殷代的礼仪,其增减多少是可以知道的。将来即或有继承周代的,虽有百个朝代,也是可以预知的。”

Zi Zhang asked: “Is it possible to forecast a country’s affairs ten ages into the future?”
Confucius answered: “The Yin Dynasty adopted the regulations of the Xia Dynasty. The modifications they made were known. The Zhou Dynasty adopted the regulations of the Yin Dynasty. The modifications they made were known. Perhaps another dynasty will take the place of Zhou Dynasty in the future. Should that keep happening, one age after another, even the affairs of one hundred ages can be predicted, too.”

孔子谓季氏,八佾舞于庭,是可忍也,
孰不可忍也?

孔子对季氏在家中举行八排歌舞(天子的礼仪)非常愤怒。他说,如果这个可以容忍,那还有什么是不可以容忍的呢?

Confucius was furious for the head of a powerful political family, Ji, using eight rows of choristers (an Imperial prerogative) in their family chapel. He said that if this could be tolerated, what else couldn't be tolerated?

定公问:"君使臣,臣事君,如之何?"
孔子对曰:"君使臣以礼,臣事君以忠。"

定公问孔子:"国君对待大臣,大臣事奉国君,如何才最适合?"
孔子说:"当国君以礼对待大臣时,大臣将以忠诚去事奉国君。"

Duke Ding asked Confucius: "How should a prince employ his ministers, and how should the ministers serve their prince?"
Confucius answered: " When the prince treats his ministers according to the rules of propriety, the ministers will serve their prince with loyalty."

三家者以《雍》彻。
子曰:"'相维辟公,天子穆穆。'奚取于三家之堂?"

三个强有力的政治家庭于祭祀完毕时歌唱《雍歌》(天子礼仪)。
孔子说:"'因为诸侯的帮助,天子的容貌看来很庄严。'这两句《诗经》上的话怎么可以在三个政治家庭的堂上唱呢?"

When Confucius heard that the three powerful political families concluded the service in their family chapels by chanting *the hymn of Yung Ode* (which could only be used by the Emperor), he said: "*The Book of Poetry* says 'Assisted by the princes, the emperor looks grave.' How could we see a service of chanting a hymn of the above sayings in these political families' chapels?"

子曰:“管仲之器小哉。”
或曰:“管仲俭乎?”
曰:“管氏有三归,官事不摄,焉得俭?”
“然则管仲知礼乎?”
曰:“邦君树塞门,管氏亦树塞门。邦君为两君之好有反坫,管氏亦有反坫。管氏而知礼孰不知礼?”

孔子说:“管仲不是一个伟大的人。”
有人问孔子:“管仲节省吗?”
孔子说:“管仲有三栋房子,并有官员负责管理,而且每一官员只管理一栋。我们如何能说管仲节省?”
这个人又问:“那么管仲知道礼仪吗?”
孔子说:“国君在宫殿门外建有短墙,管仲家门前也建有短墙。国君招待外国君主举行国宴时有特别凳子作为放置空杯之用,管仲家也有此设备。如果说管仲知道礼仪,那还有谁是不知道的呢?”

Confucius said: “Guan Zhong (a famous statesman) was not a great man.”
Some one asked: “Was Guan Zhong frugal?”
Confucius answered: “Guan Zhong had three houses and had officers to take care the affairs of houses. And each officer was in charge of only one house. How could we say Guan Zhong was frugal?”
The same person asked again: “Did Guan Zhong know the rules of propriety?”
Confucius answered: “The reigning prince had low wall built before his palace gate, and Guan Zhong also had the same. The reigning prince had special stands for placing the inverted cups when he had state dinners, and Guan Zhong had the same at his home. If we say Guan Zhong knew the rules of propriety, who did not?”

子曰："居上不宽，为礼不敬，临丧不哀，吾何以观之哉。"

孔子说："居于上位的高官对居于下位的小吏毫不宽待，行礼的时候一点也不恭敬，参加丧葬时也不表示哀伤。对于这些事情，我实在不想多看一眼。"

Confucius said: "The senior officials did not have tolerance to their junior officials. When they took part in ceremonies, they were not respectful. When they went to funerals, they did not show a sorrowful manner. I have no desire to look at such a state of things."

子曰："能以礼让为国乎，何有？不能以礼让为国，如礼何？"

孔子说："如果能以礼让为本去治理国家，那还有什么困难？如果不能，仅有那礼仪的表面文章，那又有什么用呢？"

Confucius said: "If a ruler governs his people with rules of propriety, he will have no difficulties in his work. If he does not govern this way, how can the mere rules of etiquette and formality work for him?"

子曰:"不患无位,患所以立。不患莫已知,求为可知也。"

孔子说:"不要愁没有官做,应该愁没有做官的才干。不要担心别人不知道你,应该寻求你让人知道的才能。"

Confucius said: " A person should not be concerned about not having a position; he should be concerned about how to fit himself to a position. He should not be concerned about not being known; he should seek how to deserve to be known."

子游曰:"事君数,斯辱矣。朋友数,斯疏矣。"

子游说:"事奉国君,一再地谏劝会使他不快而遭受侮辱。与朋友相处,一再劝告也会使朋友不快因而疏远。"

Zi You said: "In serving a prince, frequent advice will make the prince unhappy and brings disgrace in return. In dealing with friends, frequent advice will also make the friends unhappy and the friendship will become distant."

子使漆雕开仕。
对曰:“吾斯之未能信。”
子说。

孔子鼓励他的学生漆雕开去做官。
漆雕开回答:“我对我自己尚没有充分的信心是否能把事情做好。”
孔子对漆雕开的谦诚回答很满意。

Confucius encouraged his disciple, Qi Diaokai, to work for the government. Qi Diaokai said: “I don't have enough confidence in myself to do things well.” Confucius was pleased with Qi Diaokai's humility.

子贡问曰:“孔文子何以谓之‘文’也?”
子曰:“敏而好学,不耻下问,是以谓之‘文’也。”

子贡问孔子:“为何孔文子逝世后谥号为‘文’呢?”
孔子说:“因为他天资聪颖又很好学,向属下请教也不以为耻,所以谥号为‘文’。”

Zi Gong asked: “Why Kong Wenzi received the title of ‘WEN’ from the government after his death?”
Confucius answered: “Being fond of studies, and being not ashamed to ask and learn from the persons who are inferior to him—he deserved that title of ‘WEN’.”

孟武伯问子路仁乎。
子曰:“不知也。”
又问。
子曰:“由也,千乘之国,可使治其赋也。不知其仁也。”
“求也何如?”
子曰:“求也,千室之邑,百乘之家,可使为之宰也。不知其仁也。”
“赤也何如?”
子曰:“赤也,束带立于朝,可使与宾客言也。不知其仁也。”

孟武伯问孔子他的学生子路是否是一个仁者。
孔子说:“我不知道。”
孟武伯又问。
孔子说:“子路这个人可以管理有一千辆兵车大国的税务。可我不知道他是否是个仁者。”
孟武伯又问:“求怎么样?”
孔子说:“求这个人可以担任有一千户人家的城镇的宰官。可我不知道他是否是个仁者。”
孟武伯又问:“赤怎么样?”
孔子说:“赤这个人可以穿着礼服站在朝廷上接待宾客。可我不知道他是否是个仁者。”

Meng Wubo, a member of a powerful noble family, asked Confucius if his disciple, Zi Lu, was a man of virtue.
Confucius answered: “I don’t know.”
So the man asked again.
Confucius said: “In serving a large nation, Zi Lu is able to manage the national levies. But I don’t know if he can be called a man of virtue.”
Meng Wubo then asked: “How about Qiu?”
Confucius answered: “Qiu has the ability to take an administrative job to govern a town of one thousand families. But I don’t know if he can be called a man of virtue.”
The man then asked: “How about Chi?”
Confucius answered: “Chi can be trusted to treat the guests well in the court. But I don’t know if he can be called a man of virtue.”

子谓子产有君子之道四焉:“其行己也恭,其事上也敬,其养民也惠,其使民也义。”

孔子说子产有四点合乎君子之道:“他为人谦恭,事奉上级谨敬,对待人民有惠爱,以义理正道去使用人民。”

Confucius said of Zi Chan: “He has attained the four points of being a superior man: In conducting his personal character, he is humble; in serving his superior, he is respectful; in governing his people, he benefits them; in laboring his people, he is just.”

子曰:“晏平仲善与人交,久而敬之。”

孔子说:“晏平仲知道如何与人交往,也能长久维持友谊,保持尊敬。”

Confucius said of Yan Pingzhong: “He knows how to maintain friendship with others. He keeps his friendship long and respectful.”

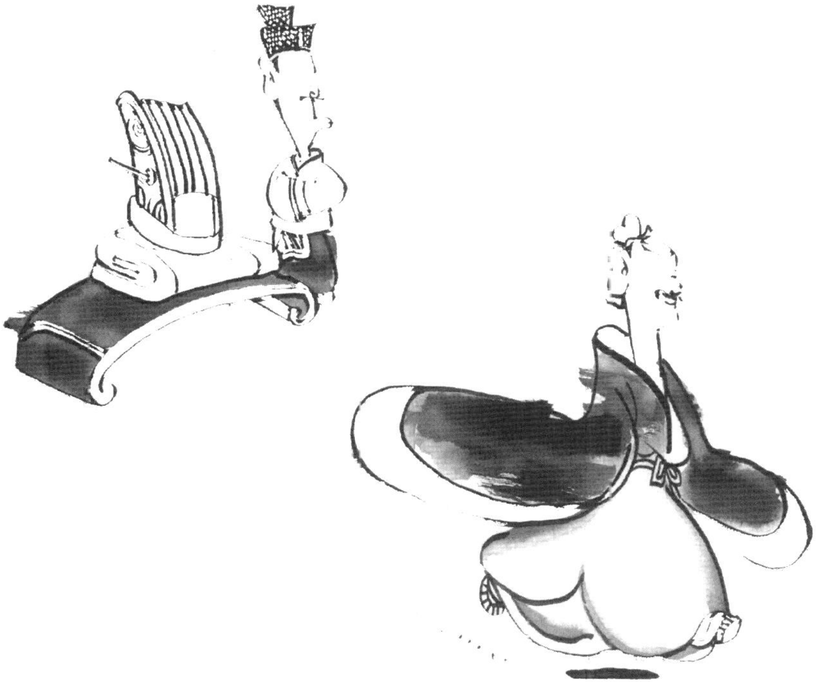

子张问曰:“令尹子文三仕为令尹,无喜色,三已之,无愠色。旧令尹之政,必以告新令尹。何如?”
子曰:“忠矣。”
曰:“仁矣乎?”
曰:“未知，焉得仁?”
“崔子弑齐君,陈文子有马十乘,弃而违之,至于他邦,则曰:‘犹吾大夫崔子也。’违之。之一邦。则又曰:‘犹吾大夫崔子也。’违之。何如?”
子曰:“清矣。”
曰:“仁矣乎?”
曰:“未知,焉得仁?”

子张问孔子:“令尹子文三次担任令尹。每次被派任时,他均没有流露出高兴的样子。每次被通知解除职务时,他也没有表示过不愉快的样子。而把他从前担任令尹时的施政情形,一定要告诉新的令尹。您认为这个人如何?”
孔子说:“算是忠诚的了。”
子张问:“是个仁者吗?”
孔子说:“我对这个人不太清楚,怎么可以知道他是个仁者呢?”
子张又问:“齐国的崔子杀了他的国君,陈文子抛弃了他的四十匹马,逃到了别的国家。说:‘这个国家的当权者和我国的崔子一样。’于是他又逃到另一个国家,说:‘这个国家的当权者和我国的崔子一样。’于是他又逃走了。您认为这个人如何?”
孔子说:“算得上是个清高的了。”
子张又问:“可以算个仁者吗?”
孔子说:“我对这个人不太清楚,怎么可以知道他是个仁者呢?”

Zi Zhang asked: “Zi Wen took the office of governor three times. Each time he was appointed, he did not display a hint of happiness. Each time he was dismissed, he did not show a hint of unhappiness, and he always told his successor what he had finished of the government policy. What do you think about the man?”
Confucius answered: “Faithful!”
Zi Zhang asked: “Could he be called a man of virtue?”
Confucius answered: “As I don’t know much about him, how could I consider him a man of virtue?”
Zi Zhang continued: “Officer Cui Zi killed his prince of Qi. Chen Wenzi abandoned his property of forty horses and left for another nation. Soon, he said, ‘The ruler in this nation is similar to our Officer Cui Zi.’ So he left again for another nation. Soon, he said, ‘The ruler in this nation is also like our Officer Cui Zi.’ Then, he left again. What do you think of Chen Wenzi?”
Confucius said: “Pure in mind.”
Zi Zhang asked again: “Could he be called a man of virtue?”
Confucius answered: “As I don’t know much about him, how could I consider him a man of virtue?”

子曰:“雍也,可使南面。”

孔子说:“雍这个人有国君的气度。”

Confucius expressed admiration for his disciple, Yong, saying: “Yong surely could occupy the place of a prince.”

子游为武城宰。
子曰:“女得人焉尔乎?”
曰:“有澹台灭明者,行不由径,非公事未尝至于偃之室也。”

子游为武城宰令。
孔子问他:“你可曾发现好人?”
子游说:“有一个人名叫澹台灭明的,他不抄捷径,除了因为公事,从不来到我的私宅。”

Zi You was the magistrate of Wu.
Confucius asked him: “Have you found good people there?”
Zi You answered: “There is a man whose name is Tantai Mieming. He has never taken a ‘short cut.’ He never came to my home unless for official business.”

仲弓问子桑伯子。
子曰:“可也,简。”
仲弓曰:“居敬而行简以临其民,不亦可乎。居简而行简,无乃太简乎?”
子曰:“雍之言然。”

仲弓问孔子子桑伯子这个人怎么样。
孔子说:“还可以,这个人做事很简约。”
仲弓说:“做人敬谨,处理政令简化,这还是可以的。如果做人简约,处理政令也很简化,那不是太简单了吗?”
孔子说:“我同意你的说法。”

Zhong Gong asked about Zisang Bozi.
Confucius said: “He may pass, but he is simple.”
Zhong Gong said: “When a man in his private life is serious, but in dealing with people, he is simple, the man should be all right. On the other hand, if he is simple in his private life, and also simple in his public life, would it be too simple?.”
Confucius said: “I agree with you.”

子华使于齐，冉子为其母请粟。
子曰："与之釜。"
请益。
曰："与之庾。"
冉子与之粟五秉。
子曰："赤之适齐也，乘肥马，衣轻裘。吾闻之也，君子周急，不继富。"
原思为之宰，与之粟九百。
辞。
子曰："毋，以与尔邻里乡党乎。"

子华出使齐国，冉子为子华的母亲向孔子要求给些米谷。
孔子说："给她六斗四升。"
冉子请增加些。
孔子说："给她十六斗吧。"事实上，冉子给了她八十斗米谷。
孔子说："子华出使齐国，乘的是匹肥壮的马，穿的是轻美的皮袄。我听说过，君子只肯济助贫人的急需，而不济助那富有的人。"
当孔子任司寇派原思为他的家臣时，孔子给他米谷九百斗，原思嫌多。
孔子说："不要嫌多，你可以分给你的乡亲邻居么。"

Zi Hua, a Confucius' disciple, was sent on a mission to Qi. Another Confucius' disciple, Ran Zi, requested grain for Zi Hua's mother who was home.
Confucius said: "Give her a quantity of Fu."
Ran requested more.
Confucius said: "Then give her a Yu."
Actually, what Ran gave to Zi Hua's mother was five Pings, much more than a Yu.
When Confucius learned about it later, he said: "I noticed that when Zi Hua was leaving, he drove in a carriage with fine horses and wore costly furs. I have heard that a superior man helps the distressed, but does not add to the rich."
When Confucius appointed another disciple, Yuan Si, as his officer, Confucius, as a senior official of the state, gave Yuan Si nine hundred measures of grain. Yuan Si declined it as too much. Confucius said: "Don't reject it. You may give some to your relatives and neighbors."

季康子问仲由可使从政也与。
子曰:“由也果,于从政乎何有?”
曰:“赐也可使从政也与?”
子曰:“赐也达,于从政乎何有?”
曰:“求也可使从政也与?”
子曰:“求也艺,于从政乎何有?”

季康子问孔子他的学生由可否从政做官。
孔子说:“由这个人做事有果断,为什么不可以从政呢?”
季康子又问:“赐可以从政做官吗?”
孔子说:“赐这个人很通达事理,为什么不可以从政呢?”
季康子又问:“求可以从政做官吗?”
孔子说:“求这个人多才多艺,为什么不可以从政呢?”

Ji Kangzi, a minister in power in Confucius' native state, asked Confucius whether his disciple, You, could be employed in the government.
Confucius answered: "You is a man who knows how to make from decisions. Why should he not become a government official?"
Ji Kangzi then asked: "Could Ci be employed in the government?"
Confucius answered: "Ci is a man of high intelligence. Why should he not become a government official?"
Ji Kangzi then asked: "Could Qiu be employed in the government?"
Confucius answered: "Qiu is a man who has many abilities. Why should he not become a government official?"

子贡曰:"如有博施于民,而能济众,何如?可谓仁乎?"
子曰:"何事于仁,必也圣乎!尧舜其犹病诸。夫仁者,己欲立而立人,己欲达而达人。能近取譬。可谓仁之方也已。"

子贡问:"如有人能广大地施惠与人民,又能救济大众,这样的人可以算是仁者吗?"
孔子说:"这不仅是仁者,简直就是圣人么!当年的尧和舜也都还没有完全做到呢。说到仁,那就是自己要立身,也要别人立身。自己要通达事理,也要别人通达事理。能就近把自身的事设想到他人。这就是达成仁道的方法。"

Zi Gong asked: "If a man could carry out extensively good works for the welfare of the people and benefit them, could such a man be called a man of virtue?"
Confucius said: "Why call him only a man of virtue? He may be called a sage. Even the ancient emperors, Yao and Shun, had not completely attained to the virtue yet. When a man of virtue is seeking to establish himself, he also seeks to establish others; when he is wishing to enlighten himself, he also wishes to enlighten others. Taking the example of himself, he would think of others. Those are how to practice virtue."

子谓颜渊曰:“用之则行,舍之则藏,惟我与尔有是夫。”
子路曰:“子行三军则谁与?”
子曰:“暴虎冯河,死而无悔者,吾不与也。必也临事而惧,好谋而成者也。”

孔子对颜渊说:“如有国君用我,我就实行我所信奉的正道。如果不用我,我就退隐。只有你和我有这种工夫吧。”
子路听到他的老师赞美颜渊,他问道:“如果老师去统率三军,你将和谁一同去呢?”
孔子说:“仗着勇敢,空手去打老虎,溺水过河,到死也不后悔的人,我是不取的。我将带这个人同去,在大战临头时,他知道如何妥为筹划,运用战略,赢战役。”

Confucius said to Yan Yuan, “When called to office, we accept the jobs; if not, we retire without regret. Only we, two, can do it naturally.”
Confucius' another disciple, Zi Lu, heard of his master's praise of Yan Yuan. He asked, “If you were in charge of a great army, whom would you take with you ?”
Confucius said: “I would not take the man who wanted to fight against a tiger with his bare hands, or to jump into water to cross a river without fear of death. I would take the man who knows how to plan deliberately and use strategy to win a battle.”

曾子有疾,孟敬子问之。
曾子言曰:"鸟之将死,其鸣也哀;人之将死,其言也善。君子所贵乎道者三:动容貌,斯远暴慢矣;正颜色,斯近信矣;出辞气,斯远鄙倍矣。笾豆之事,则有司存。"

曾子生了重病,孟敬子去探视他。
曾子说:"当一只鸟将死时,它的鸣声是很悲哀的。人在将死时,他的话语也是善良的。君子看重的德行有下面三点:他的举动要温和,就会远离粗鲁;他的脸色要端庄,就会使人觉得他有诚信;他的说话声调要适中,就不会使人觉得轻浮。其他的礼节方面,让各职司人员去做。"

Confucius' disciple, Zeng Zi, was critically ill. A young noble friend, Meng Jingzi, came to visit him. Zeng Zi said: "When a bird is going to die, its singing is sad. When a man is going to die, his words are good. A superior man emphasizes the following three things: His deportment must be gentle so he can keep away from violence. His countenance must be sincere so people will believe he is faithful. His tone of voice must be moderate so people will not think his words are mean. As for the other details, the officials in charge will take care of them."

曾子曰:“可以托六尺之孤,可以寄百里之命,临大节而不可夺也,君子人与?君子人也!”

曾子说:“在国君将过世时,可以把辅助幼君的重任交托给他,可以把百里小国的政事叫他总揽而临到重要关头也不会变节。这样的一个人可以叫做君子吗?是的,可以叫做真正的君子!”

Zeng Zi said: “If a man could be entrusted by a dying prince to take care of his soon-to-be orphaned prince, and also to be in charge of the national political affairs on behalf of the orphaned prince, and nothing could drive him away from his principles, could the man be called a superior man? Yes, he would be a real superior man!”

子曰："民可使由之，不可使知之。"

孔子说："一般人民只能告诉他们如何去做，不可以使他们了解为何要如此做。"

Confucius said: " The common people can be directed how to do things, but they can not be made to understand the reasons why."

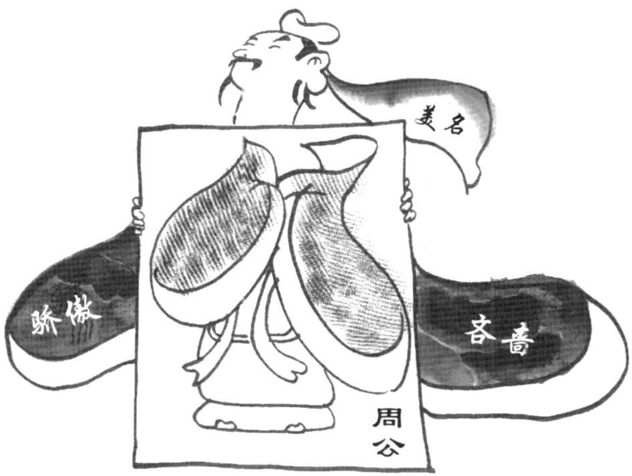


子曰："如有周公之才之美，使骄且吝，其余不足观也已。"

孔子说："即或这个人有当年周公的美名，如果他是骄傲而又吝啬，他的其余部分也就不足一观了。"

Confucius said: " Even though a man may have abilities as admirable as those of the former Duke of Zhou, if he is proud and miserly, his other qualities are not worthy of checking."

子曰:“笃信好学,守死善道。危邦不入,乱邦不居。天下有道则见,无道则隐。邦有道,贫且贱焉,耻也。邦无道,富且贵焉,耻也。”

孔子说:“一个人应当诚笃信实去追求学问,要服膺正道一直到死。不去政治不稳定的国家,不住危乱的国家。天下有道的时候出来行道,天下无道时就退隐。国家政治清明时,如仍是贫穷低贱,那就是耻辱。国家政治不清明时,反而是既富且贵,那也是耻辱。”

Confucius said: “A man should study faithfully and diligently. He should keep learning the truth until death. Don't enter a nation if it is in danger, and don't live in a nation if it is in chaos. If the nation is well governed, go work for the government. If the nation is ill governed, retire. If the nation is in order, but you are still poor and hold a mean position, that is a shame. If the nation is not in order, and you are rich and hold a high position in the government, that is a shame, too.”

子曰:“不在其位,不谋其政。”

孔子说:“不在这个职位上,就不要过问这个职位所管的政事。”

Confucius said: “If a man is not holding a certain position in the government, he should not handle the political affairs which belong to that position.”

子曰:“大哉,尧之为君也。巍巍乎,唯天为大,唯尧则之。荡荡乎,民无能名焉。巍巍乎其有成功也,焕乎其有文章。”

孔子说:“尧真是一位伟大的国君。假如天是最伟大的,尧的伟大可以和天相比美。因为他太伟大了,人民不知道如何去赞美他。他的成就是宏伟的。他所订立的规章是好得无以复加的。”

Confucius said: “Great indeed was Yao as a ruler of the empire. If the Heaven was the greatest, his ruling would be as great as the Heaven. He was so great that the people did not even know how to praise him. His accomplishments were great. The regulations which he instituted were glorious.”

子曰:“禹,吾无间然矣。菲饮食,而致孝乎鬼神。恶衣服,而致美乎黻冕。卑宫室,而尽力乎沟洫。禹,吾无间然矣。”

孔子说:“对于大禹王,我是找不出任何瑕疵可以批评的了。他自己的饮食很简单,可是他在祭祀鬼神上所用的祭品却很丰美。他本人平时所穿的衣服很粗糙,可是在祭祀时所穿戴的却很精美。他自己所住的宫室很简陋,可是他尽力去修建水道。因此对于大禹王,我是没有半点可以指责的了。”

Confucius said: “I can find no flaw in the character of the ancient emperor, the Great Yu. He ate simple foods, but he offered lavish ones to the spirits. He wore coarse clothes, but when he attended a worship, he wore refined clothes. The palace where he lived was humble and plain, but he spent a great amount on the ditches and water channels. Therefore, I can find no flaw in the Great Yu.”

朝,与下大夫言,侃侃如也。与上大夫言,訚訚如也。君在,踧踖如也,与与如也。

在朝廷上,孔子与地位较低的官员谈话时很坦诚率直。与地位较高的官员讲话时是和气沉着。如果国君在场,他的态度是恭敬的,也很镇静。

In court with the lower officials, Confucius spoke freely in a straightforward manner. With the senior officials, he spoke kindly, but with self-possession. If the prince was present, Confucius was respectful, but also composed.

侍食于君,君祭,先饭。

当孔子奉命与国君一同吃饭时,孔子必先代国君尝食,然后由国君祭祖,祭完了方才食用。

Whenever Confucius was ordered to eat with the prince, he would taste the food for the prince to see whether it was all right, before the prince offered the food for sacrifice. After that, they ate.

君召使摈，色勃如也，足躩如也。揖所与立，左右手，衣前后，襜如也。趋进，翼如也。宾退，必复命曰："宾不顾矣。"

当国君要孔子去送走重要的宾客时，孔子的态度就会立刻振作起来，脚步也加快了。然后，向左右前后的同事鞠躬，整衣冠，快步上前，以尊严从容的步伐陪同宾客前行。当宾客辞退了时，孔子就会向国君报告："宾客已经走远了。"

When the prince called Confucius to bid an important visitor farewell, Confucius would change his countenance immediately and walk a little bit faster. Then bow right and left to the officers in attendance, adjust the folds of his robes, quicken his steps, and walk out with the visitor with dignity and ease. When the visitor had left, Confucius would report to the prince, "The visitor has departed."

入公门，鞠躬如也，如不容。立不中门，行不履阈。过位，色勃如也，足躩如也，其言似不足者。摄齐升堂，鞠躬如也，屏气似不息者。出，降一等，逞颜色，怡怡如也。没阶，趋进，翼如也。复其位，踧踖如也。

当孔子走进国君的大门时，他会低下身子，就好像门太矮而不能直立的样子。他不会站立在门的当中，走路也不会踏着门坎。走过国君坐的空位子时，态度恭敬，就好像国君仍坐在那儿。行走文雅，讲话声音很低，就好像是气不足似的。提起衣襟走向内殿，低下身子，屏住气息，就好像没有气息似的。退出时，等到下了一级台阶，脸色立刻转为平和。下完了台阶向前走时，脚步就快了。走回自己的位子后，保持着恭敬不安的神态。

When Confucius was entering into the door of prince's palace, he would bend low as if it were not high enough for him to admit. He would not stand in the middle of the door, nor step on the doorsill. When he was passing by the vacant seat of the prince, he would walk attentively and speak only in whispers as if the prince were sitting there. When he was ascending the steps to the reception hall, he would hold his robe up with both hands, his body bent, holding his breath, as if he dared not breathe. After the audience, when he was descending, as soon as he had walked down one step, he would relax his countenance and look satisfied. When he had arrived at the bottom of the steps, he would rapidly return to his position and kept a manner of respectful uneasiness.

执圭，鞠躬如也，如不胜。上如揖，下如授，勃如战色，足蹜蹜如有循。享礼，有容色；私觌，愉愉如也。

拿着国君的圭玉时，态度恭敬谨慎，像拿不动的样子。拿得高时像在作揖，拿得低时，像给人家东西似的，容色是既庄且敬。移步时，脚尖稍起，后跟不离地，好像是循着什么走似的。到了礼节完毕时，容色舒畅。等到行私见礼时，容色便显得和悦多了。

When Confucius was carrying the scepter of his prince, he would bend his body as if the weight of the scepter were too heavy for him to carry, holding it not higher than his forehead, nor lower than his chest. He looked apprehensive, walking along slowly as if his feet were heavy. After presenting the gifts with which he was charged, he would wear a placid expression. During his private audience, he would look highly pleased.

康子馈药，拜而受之，曰：“丘未达，不敢尝。”

季康子送孔子药，孔子拜着受下了，说：“因为我还不懂这个药性，所以不敢立刻就吃。”

When Ji Kangzi, a minister in power in Confucius' state, sent Confucius a gift of medicine, Confucius accepted it with a bow, saying: "I do not know the nature of the medicine, so I'll not take it now."

君赐食，必正席，先尝之。君赐腥，必熟而荐之。君赐生，必畜之。

如果国君赐给孔子煮熟的食物，孔子收到后，必先端坐好，亲自尝了，然后才分给别人去吃。如国君送给孔子尚未煮熟的生肉，一定要将之煮熟了，先祭奉祖先，然后再吃。如果国君送给孔子一头畜生，孔子一定先把它养起来。

Whenever the prince sent Confucius a gift of cooked food, Confucius would adjust his mat and sit on it, then taste it before letting others eat. Whenever the prince sent Confucius a gift of uncooked meat, he would have it cooked and offer some to the spirits of his ancestors before eating it. Whenever the prince sent Confucius a living animal as a gift, he would keep it alive.

疾,君视之。东首,加朝服拖绅。

当孔子生病了,国君来看他时,孔子将会把头朝向东方,穿上朝服,拖着大带子。

Whenever Confucius was sick and his prince came to see him, he would lie with his head toward the east, with his court uniform over him and the belt across the uniform.

君命召,不俟驾,行矣。

当国君召见孔子时,孔子不等车子驾好了就走。

Whenever Confucius received a summon from his prince, he would dress up immediately and go without waiting for the carriage to come.

入太庙，每事问。

当孔子进入太庙陪祭时，遇到任何不懂的地方，他都会问个明白。

Whenever Confucius was attending the ancestral temple of the state, he would ask about everything which he did not understand.

# 国库

鲁人为长府。
闵子骞曰:“仍旧贯，如之何，何必改作?”
子曰:“夫人不言，言必有中。”

鲁国的人要重新做一个国库。
闵子骞说:“旧的仍然可用，何必要做个新的?”
孔子说:“这个人不常说话，可每次说的都有道理。”

Some people in the state of Lu tried to build a new building as the national treasury.
Confucius' disciple, Ming Ziqian, said: “The old building is still all right. Why do they have to build a new one?”
When Confucius heard of the talk, he said: “That man seldom speaks. Once he speaks, he always hits the point.”

季氏富于周公，而求也为之聚敛而附益之。
子曰："非吾徒也。小子鸣鼓而攻之可也。"

季氏的财富居然超过了当年的宰相周公，而孔子的弟子求竟仍帮助季氏去敛财。
孔子对他的其他弟子们说："求不再有资格做我的学生了，你们可以去攻击他。"

A noble of the Ji family was richer than the early premier, Zhou Gong. Confucius' disciple, Qiu, worked for the noble and helped his master collect wealth to make the noble richer.
Confucius said to his other disciples: "Qiu is not qualified as my disciple any more. You may attack him."

季子然问:"仲由、冉求可谓大臣与?"
子曰:"吾以子为异之问,曾由与求之问。所谓大臣者,以道事君,不可,则止。今由与求也,可谓具臣矣。"
曰:"然则从之者与?"
子曰:"弑父与君,亦不从也。"

季子然问孔子:"仲由和冉求可以算大臣吗?"
孔子说:"我以为你问什么别的问题,原来是问仲由和冉求。所谓大臣,应该以正道去辅助国君,如果国君不听从,就应该辞职。如今仲由与冉求两个人,也不过是一般的臣子罢了。"
季子然又问:"那么他们是对国君绝对服从的了?"
孔子说:"那也不见得。如果国君要去杀害父亲和天子,他们也不会服从的。"

Ji Ziran, a member of a powerful noble family, asked Confucius: "Could Zhong You and Ran Qiu be listed as great ministers?"
Confucius answered: "A great minister must serve his prince in the right way. If the prince does not take his advice, he should resign. Today, Zhong You and Ran Qiu may only be called ordinary ministers."
Ji Ziran asked: "Does it mean that they always follow their prince's commands?"
Confucius answered: "Not exactly, of course. If their prince wanted them to commit parricide or regicide, they would not obey him."

子路使子羔为费宰。
子曰:“贼夫人之子。”
子路曰:“有民人焉,有社稷焉,何必读书,然后为学。”
子曰:“是故恶夫佞者。”

子路帮助子羔成为费邑的地方官。
孔子说:“你这是去害人家的儿子。”
子路说:“有人民去给他治理,有宗庙去给他祭祀,何必一定要读书才算学习呢?”
孔子说:“所以我最恨强词夺理的人。”

Zi Lu arranged Zi Gao to be appointed as the magistrate of Fei, so the young man had to quit school.
Confucius said: “You are injuring a person’s son.”
Zi Lu replied: “He will have people to deal with. He will have the ancestral temple to serve. Why should he keep studying the books in order to learn?”
Confucius said: “That is the reason why I hate the people who like to argue.”

# 信

子贡问政。
子曰:“足食,足兵,民信之矣。”
子贡曰:“必不得已而去,于斯三者何先?”
曰:“去兵。”
子贡曰:“必不得已而去,于斯二者何先?”
曰:“去食。自古皆有死,民无信不立。”

子贡问孔子如何从政治国。
孔子说:“必须有充足的粮食和充足的军队,还要使人民对政府有信心。”
子贡又问:“如果必须去掉一种,在这三者中应该去哪一种?”
孔子说:“去掉军队。”
子贡又问:“如果必须再去掉一种,在这两者中应该去掉哪一种?”
孔子说:“去掉粮食。自古以来每个人都要死的。如果人民对政府没有信心了,那么这个政府便不能存在了。”

Zi Gong asked about politics.
Confucius said: “To provide sufficient food for the people, to keep an efficient army for the nation, and to let people have faith in the government.”
Zi Gong asked: “If, or some reason, one of the three factors must be eliminated, which one must go?”
Confucius said: “The army.”
Zi Gong asked again: “If, for some reason, one of the other two must be eliminated, which one must go?”
“The food,” Confucius answered. “Everybody will die. If the people have no faith in their government, the government will not be able to exist.”

棘子成曰:“君子质而已矣,何以文为?”
子贡曰:“惜乎夫子之说君子也?驷不及舌。文犹质也,质犹文也。虎豹之鞟，犹犬羊之鞟也。”

棘子成问子贡:“君子只要有实质就好了,何必要那外表的文采呢?”
子贡说:“你怎么可以这样说君子呢?一个人话说出口后,就是乘着四匹马拉的车子也追不上的。要知道外面的文采和里面的实质是同样地重要。如果不注重表里,那就同去掉毛之后,虎豹之皮与犬羊之皮一样,是分辨不出来的。”

Ji Zicheng, an official, said to Zi Gong: “A superior man seeks only the substantial qualities. Why does he need to seek the ornamental accomplishments?”
Zi Gong replied: “How could you say a superior man like that? Once a person’s words have been spoken out, they can never be taken back, not even by pulling a carriage with four horses. The ornamental accomplishments are as important as the substantial qualities. Without both, it will be like that, after taking the hairs off, the hide of a tiger or a leopard will look the same as that of a dog or a goat.”

哀公问于有若曰:“年饥,用不足,如之何?”
有若对曰:“盍彻乎?”
曰:“二,吾犹不足,如之何其彻也?”
对曰:“百姓足,君孰与不足?百姓不足,君孰与足?”

哀公问有若:“如今年岁饥荒,政府的税收不足以支出,怎么办?”
有若说:“为什么不收十分之一的税?”
哀公说:“当前的税收是十分之二,我还嫌不足,怎么可以只收十分之一的税呢?”
有若说:“如果百姓富足,国君怎么会不富足?如果百姓不富足,国君怎么可能富足呢?”

Duke Ai, asked You Ruo: “This is a year of famine. The revenues received do not meet the expenses. What can we do?”
You Ruo replied: “Why don’t you tax at one-tenth?”
Duke Ai said: “We are taxing at two-tenths right now, and we still run short of paying our expenses. How can we tax at one-tenth?”
You Ruo said: “If the people have plenty, how can the prince not have plenty? If the people do not have plenty, how can the prince have plenty?”

齐景公问政于孔子。
对曰:“君君臣臣,父父子子。”
公曰:“善哉。信如君不君,臣不臣,父不父,子不子,虽有粟,吾得而食诸?”

齐景公问孔子为政治国的大道理。
孔子说:“做国君的要像个国君的样子,做臣子的要像个臣子的样子,做父亲的要像个父亲的样子,做儿子的要像个儿子的样子。”
齐景公说:“你说得对。如果国君不像个国君,臣子不像个臣子,父亲不像个父亲,儿子不像个儿子,那我虽然仍有收入,还能安然享受吗?”

The reigning prince of the State of Qi, Duke Jing, asked how to govern a nation well.
Confucius replied: “In order to govern well, the prince must act like a prince; each minister must act like a minister; each father must act like a father, and each son must act like a son.”
Duke Jing said: “You are absolutely right. If the prince does not act like a prince; a minister does not act like a minister; a father does not act like a father; and a son does not act like a son; although I still have my income, how could I enjoy it?”

子张问政。
子曰:“居之无倦,行之以忠。”

子张问孔子如何办理政务。
孔子说:“执行职务时不要懈怠,更要有忠诚之心。”

Zi Zhang asked how to serve best in the government.
Confucius replied: “An official should not be tired of performing his official duties. Furthermore, when he is performing, he must be faithful.”

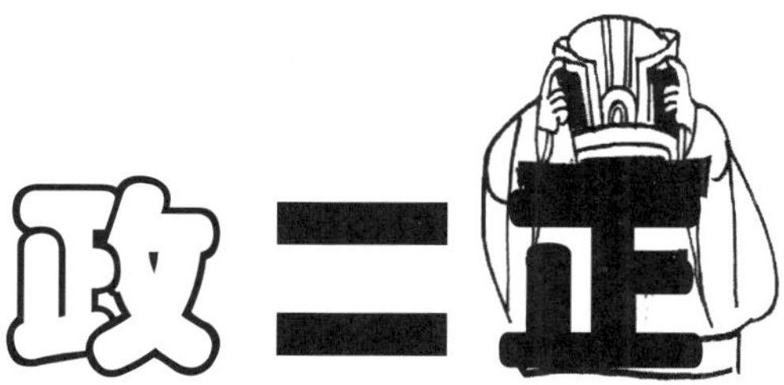


季康子问政于孔子。
孔子对曰:“政者正也。子帅以正,孰敢不正?”

季康子问孔子如何办理政务。
孔子说:“政的意义就是正。如果你能率先从事正道,那么还有谁敢不从事正道呢?”

A noble, also a minister in power in Confucius' native state, Ji Kangzi, asked Confucius how to govern the people.
Confucius replied: “Governing means correction. If you do things according to the principles of correction, how dare the people not do things accordingly?”

季康子患盗，问于孔子。
孔子对曰:“苟子之不欲，虽赏之不窃。”

季康子以其国内多盗为忧，问孔子该如何办理。
孔子说:“假如你没有贪念，人民会跟随你也没有贪念。到那个时候，就是你去鼓励他们偷盗，他们也不会做的。”

Ji Kangzi was irritated about the growing number of thieves in the state, asking Confucius how to decrease the number.
Confucius replied: “If you were not greedy, people would follow your good example not to be greedy. Under such circumstances, even though you tried to reward the people to steal, they would not do it.”

季康子问政于孔子,曰:"如杀无道,以就有道,何如?"
孔子对曰:"子为政,焉用杀?子欲善,而民善矣。君子之德,风;小人之德,草。草上之风,必偃。"

季康子问孔子如何办理政务。他问孔子:"如果把那些不好的人杀掉来保护好人,你认为如何?"
孔子回答道:"掌理国政不要用杀的方法。如果你去做善事,人民自然会跟着你去向善的。君子的行为像风一样,小人的行为像草一样。风一吹,草定会随着倒下的。"

Ji Kangzi asked Confucius about governing the people, saying: "How about using the method of killing the bad people to protect the good ones?"
Confucius replied: "Governing does not mean killing. If you do good deeds, the people will follow you with good deeds. The officials' conduct is like the wind and the people's conduct is like the grasses. When the wind blows, the grasses will bend."

子路问政。
子曰:“先之,劳之。”
请益。
曰:“无倦。”

子路问孔子如何从政。
孔子说:“凡事要自身先做个好的榜样,而且要勤劳。”
子路请再多说一些。
孔子说:“还要不能厌倦。”

Zi Lu asked how to govern the people.
Confucius replied: “First, you must set a good example to do whatever you would like them to do. Furthermore, you must do it diligently.”
Zi Lu requested more advice.
Confucius said: “Whatever you do, you must not get weary of doing it.”

仲弓为季氏宰，问政。
子曰："先有司，赦小过，举贤才。"
曰："焉知贤才而举之？"
曰："举尔所知，尔所不知，人其舍诸？"

仲弓为季氏的总管，请教孔子如何去管理。
孔子说："先监督各部门的主管，遇到有人犯了小的过错时就饶恕他，举用那些有德行的人。"
仲弓问："我如何知道哪些人有德行呢？"
孔子说："举用那些你所已经知道的。那些你尚不知道的，难道别人会舍弃他吗？"

Zhong Gong, being appointed as the chief administrator of the powerful Ji family, asked Confucius how to deal with the staff who worked under him.
Confucius replied: "Supervise your department heads first. Pardon the small faults and advance the men of good conduct and abilities."
Zhong Gong asked: "How do I know which one has good conduct and abilities?"
Confucius answered: "Advance the ones you have discovered. As for the one whom you have not discovered, will the other people not let you know him?"

子路曰:“卫君待子而为政,子将奚先?”
子曰:“必也正名乎。”
子路曰:“有是哉?子之迂也。奚为正?”
子曰:“野哉由也。君子于其所不知,盖阙如也。名不正,则言不顺;言不顺,则事不成;事不成,则礼乐不兴;礼乐不兴,则刑罚不中;刑罚不中,则民无所措手足。故君子名之必可言也,言之必可行也。君子于其言无所苟而已矣。”

子路问孔子:“如果卫国国君请你去主持国政,你将从哪一方面着手?”
孔子说:“我将首先去正名分。”
子路说:“有这个道理吗?您真是太迂腐了。为什么要去正名分呢?”
孔子说:“你真粗野。君子对于自己不知道的,就暂时放在一边,不妄加反对。要知道名分不正,说话就不顺理。说话不顺理,事情就不容易办成功。事情办不成功,礼仪就不会兴旺。礼仪不兴旺,刑罚就不会用得适当。刑罚用得不适当,老百姓就凡事都不知道如何办才好。所以君子认为立好名分必须在道理上可以说得过去,如此才可以行得通。因此,君子说话是不应该不小心的。”

Zi Lu asked Confucius: “If the prince of the state of Wei asked you to govern his nation for him, what would you do first?”
Confucius said: “If that happened to me, I would define the governmental positions first.”
Zi Lu said: “Is that so? You are indeed impractical. What do we need to define the positions for?”
Confucius said: “You are rude. A superior man would not say something carelessly if he did not understand the issue very well. If a position were not defined, the man who occupied that position would not speak properly. If his speeches were not proper, things would not be done smoothly. If things were not done smoothly, the proprieties would not flourish. If the proprieties would not flourish, the punishments would not be given correctly. If the punishments were not given correctly, the people would not know what to do. Therefore, a superior man wants to define the positions in a reasonable and practical way. A superior man must not speak carelessly.”

子曰:“其身正,不令而行;其身不正,虽令不从。”

孔子说:“在上位的人如果自身做事正直,虽然不下命令,人民也会服从的。如果在上位的人,自身不按正道去做,则他虽然下命令,人民也不会服从的。”

Confucius said: “If the officials do things properly, even if they don’t give orders, the people will be submissive. If the officials do not do things properly, even if they give orders, the people will not be submissive.”

子曰:“鲁卫之政,兄弟也。”

孔子说:“鲁国和卫国的政治情况相近,真就好像兄弟一样。”

Confucius said: “The politics of the state of Lu and the state of Wei are as similar as two brothers.”

子谓卫公子荆善居室。始有曰:“苟合矣。”少有曰:“苟完矣。”富有曰:“苟美矣。”

孔子说卫国公子荆最会理财了。起初刚有点钱时,他就说:“可以够了。”等有了多点钱时,他就说:“足够了。”到他真正富有了,他就说:“真是太美满了。”

Confucius said that Jing, an official of the state of Wei, really knew how to manage the financial affairs. When he just started to have a little income, he would say, “I have enough.” When he had a little more, he would say, “I have plenty.” When he had much more, he would say, “It is perfect now.”

子曰:“苟有用我者,期月而已可也。三年有成。”

孔子说:“假如有个国君任用我去为他主理国政,一年后就可以有成绩。三年后将会使国家大治。”

Confucius said: “If I were employed to conduct the government affairs by a prince, in one year, I could accomplish something. In three years, I could have the nation in exceptional order.”

子适卫,冉有仆。子曰:“庶矣哉。”
冉有曰:“既庶矣,又何加焉?”
曰:“富之。”
曰:“既富矣,又何加焉?”
曰:“教之。”

孔子到卫国去,冉有替他驾车。当孔子看到了这么多人时,不由说道:“人真多啊。”
冉有说:“百姓这么众多,政府应该做些什么呢?”
孔子说:“使他们富足。”
冉有又问:“都富足了,又做什么呢?”
孔子说:“教育他们。”

When Confucius went to the state of Wei, his disciple, Ran You, was driving his carriage. Noticing that there were many people in Wei, Confucius said: “What a large population lives here!”
Ran You asked: “Since there is such a large population, what should the government do for the people?”
Confucius answered: “Make them rich.”
Ran You asked: “What is the next thing after making them rich?”
Confucius answered: “Educate them.”

子曰:“善人为邦百年,亦可以胜残去杀矣。诚哉是言也。”

孔子说:“有人说如果一直有诚恳的好人来治理国家一百年,就可以使残暴消失,死刑也将不需要了。这话是对的。”

Confucius said: “It is said that if we could always have good and honest men to conduct the government affairs for a period of one hundred years, violence would disappear, and capital punishment would not be needed. I agree.”

子曰:“如有王者,必世而后仁。”

孔子说:“如果有一个能行王道的人去治理国家,也要等一世之久才可以达到仁的境界。”

Confucius said: “If a kind and just ruler began to rule the nation, it could still take a whole generation before virtue started to prevail.”

冉子退朝。
子曰:“何晏也?”
对曰:“有政。”
子曰:“其事也。如有攻,虽不吾以,吾其与闻之。”

冉子从办公处回来。
孔子问他:“怎么这么晚才回来?”
冉子说:“有公事处理。”
孔子说:“可能是私事吧。如果是朝廷公事,虽然我不在朝廷服务,我还是会被咨询的。”

Confucius' disciple, Ran Zi, returned from the government office.
Confucius asked: “Why did you come back so late?”
Ran Zi answered: “We had state affairs to do at the office.”
Confucius said: “I am afraid you had personal affairs to do. If there were state affairs, even though I am not employed by the government, I might still be consulted.”

子曰:“苟正其身矣,于从政乎何有?不能正其身,如正人何?”

孔子说:“如果一个人自身的行为已经达于正道,那他还会有什么困难去从事政治呢?如果这个人自身的行为都没有达到正道,他如何可以去管理别人?”

Confucius said: “If a man could put his own conduct in good order, how could he not put the government affairs in good order? If his own conduct is not in good order, how could he correct other people whose conducts are not in good order?”

定公问:"一言而可以兴邦,有诸?"
孔子对曰:"言不可以若是其几也。人之言曰:'为君难,为臣不易。'如知为君之难也,不几乎一言而兴邦乎?"
曰:"一言而丧邦,有诸?"
孔子对曰:"言不可以若是其几也。人之言曰:'予无乐乎为君,唯其言而莫予违也。'如其善而莫之违也,不亦善乎。如不善而莫之违也,不几乎一言而丧邦乎?"

定公问孔子:"一句话可以使国家兴盛,有这个道理吗?"
孔子回答:"一句话不会如此严重的。不过,有句俗话说:'做个国君是件难事。做个臣子也不是容易事。'如果国君能够知道做国君是件难事,他就会尽心去做好。那不就是几乎一句话可以使国家兴盛了么?"
定公又问:"一句话可以使一个国家败坏,有这个道理吗?"
孔子说:"一句话不会如此严重的。不过,有句俗话说:'除了没有人敢反对我的话外,做国君实在没有什么好玩的。'如果国君的话都是好话,没有人去反对,这当然好。如果国君的话不是好话,而没有人敢去反对,那不就是几乎一句话可以使国家败坏了么?"

Duke Ding, the reigning prince of Confucius' native state, asked: "Is there such a saying as 'One single sentence can make a nation prosperous?' "
Confucius replied: "One sentence can not make a nation prosperous. However, an old saying says, 'It is difficult to be a prince, and it is not easy to be a minister, either.' If a prince really knew it was difficult to be a prince, he would try his best to be a good prince. In that case, doesn't it mean that one sentence can almost make a nation prosperous?"
Duke Ding asked again: "Is there such a saying as 'One single sentence can ruin a nation?' "
Confucius replied: "One sentence can not ruin a nation. However, an old saying says, 'Except that nobody dares disobey my orders, I don't think that being a prince is a happy thing.' If a prince's orders were always good, and nobody dared disobey him, that would be wonderful. If a prince's orders were not good, and nobody dared disobey him, doesn't it mean that one sentence can almost ruin a nation?"

子夏为莒父宰，问政。
子曰："无欲速，无见小利。欲速则不达，见小利则大事不成。"

子夏作了莒父的地方官，问孔子如何去治理。孔子说："做事不要要求很快就可以完成，不要贪图小的便宜。如果求快有时候事情反会不成功。如果贪图小便宜，大事就办不成了。"

Zi Xia, a disciple of Confucius, being appointed as the magistrate of Ju Fu, asked his master how to govern the People.
Confucius said: "Do not expect to finish a project too quickly, and do not take small advantages. If you try to finish a project too quickly, sometimes, it just can not be done. If you want to take small advantages, a great mission will not be accomplished."

叶公问政。
子曰："近者说，远者来。"

叶公问孔子如何治理政务。
孔子说："使居住近的人喜悦，那么居住远的人民就会来归了。"

Duke Ye asked Confucius how to govern a nation. Confucius answered: "Make the people nearby happy. Then people from faraway will all come and stay."

叶公语孔子曰:“吾党有直躬者。其父攘羊,而子证之。”
孔子曰:“吾党之直躬者异于是。父为子隐,子为父隐。直在其中矣。”

叶公告诉孔子说:“我家乡有个正直人。他的父亲偷了人家的羊,他去作证。”
孔子说:“我家乡的正直人与你那儿的人不同。父亲替儿子隐瞒错事,儿子替父亲隐瞒错事。正直就在其中了。”

Duke Ye said to Confucius: “We have an honest man in our area. When his father stole a sheep, he appeared to be the witness.”
Confucius said: “The honest people in our area are different from the one in your area. The father tries to hide his son’s wrongdoing, and the son also tries to hide his father’s wrongdoing. Our honesty is found in this kind of action.”

子贡问曰:“何如斯可谓之士矣?”
子曰:“行己有耻,使于四方,不辱君命。可谓士矣。”
曰:“敢问其次。”
曰:“宗族称孝焉,乡党称弟焉。”
曰:“敢问其次。”
曰:“言必信,行必果,硁硁然小人哉,抑亦可以为次矣。”

子贡问:“怎样才可以叫做士?”
孔子说:“端正自己的行为并有廉耻心,被派出使外国时,不会辱没国君的使命,这种人可以叫做士了。”
子贡又问:“那次一等的人呢?”
孔子说:“在宗族里大家说他孝顺父母,在乡里间,人人说他友爱兄弟。”
子贡又问:“那再次一等的人呢?”
孔子说:“说话有信用,做事有决断;虽然看起来不太重要,但也可以算是再次一等的人了。”

Zi Gong asked: “What are the qualities of a scholar?”
Confucius said: “His personal conduct is just and he has a shameful sense if he does something wrong. When he is sent to a foreign nation as a representative, he will not disgrace his commission. Such a man can be called a scholar.”
Zi Gong than asked: “What would be the next important qualities?”
Confucius said: “When he stays at home, his families and relatives all say he is filial to his parents. In the village, the villagers all say he is fraternal with others.”
Zi Gong then asked again: “What would be the next qualities?”
Confucius said: “He always carries out what he promised. He always finishes what he started. Although it may sound not very important, I think they would belong to the next qualities.”

子曰:“以不教民战,是谓弃之。”

孔子说:“把没有受过军事训练的人送上战场,等于是送死。”

Confucius said: “To send untrained people to war is to send them to be killed.”

子曰:“君子易事而难说也。说之不以道,不说也。及其使人也,器之。小人难事而易说也。说之虽不以道,说也。及其使人也,求备焉。”

孔子说:“君子容易侍候,不容易取悦,如果不以正道去取悦他,他是不会高兴的,当他去用人时,他将适才而用。小人很难侍候,可容易取悦,当取悦他时虽然不用正道,他也会高兴的。等到他去使用人时,他却会处处求全责备。”

Confucius said: “A superior man is easy to serve, but difficult to please. If you try to please him but do not use the proper way, he will not be pleased. When he employs people, he selects them according to their abilities. An inferior man is difficult to serve, but easy to please. If you try to please him, even if you do not use the proper way, he will still be pleased. When he employs people, he expects them to do everything.”

南宫适问于孔子曰:"羿善射,奡荡舟,俱不得其死然。禹、稷躬稼而有天下。"
夫子不答。
南宫适出,子曰:"君子哉若人。尚德哉若人。"

南宫适对孔子说:"以前的羿很会射箭,奡的力气大得可以在陆地上荡舟。可是,他们都没有好死。禹和稷原来都是农夫,可他们后来都统治天下。"
孔子没有回答。
等到南宫适走出去了,孔子对其他的学生称赞南宫适说:"真是一个君子,真是有仁德的人。"

Nan Gongshi said to Confucius: "The former ruler, Yi, was skillful at archery. Another former ruler, Rao, could move a boat on land. Neither of the two men died a natural death. Two other former rulers, Yu and Ji, had worked in the field as farmers, and they later became good rulers of nation."
Confucius did not say anything.
After Nan Gongshi left the room, Confucius praised Nan Gongshi to his other disciples: "What a superior man he is. He is a man who pursues virtue."

子路问成人。
子曰:“若臧武仲之知,公绰之不欲,卞庄子之勇,冉求之艺,文之以礼乐,亦可以为成人矣。”
曰:“今之成人者何必然,见利思义,见危授命,久要不忘平生之言,亦可以为成人矣。”

子路问孔子怎样才可以叫做完美的人。
孔子说:“如若有像臧武仲的知识,公绰的清廉无私,卞庄子的勇敢,冉求的多才多艺,再加上中和有节的礼乐陶养,这个人就可以称之为完美的人了。”
接着孔子又说:“现在的所谓完美的人是没有这样完备的。只要是见到了利益还能想到义理,临到危难时能不惜生命,和人相约,不论多久都不会忘记,如能做到这些,也可以叫做完美的人了。”

Zi Lu asked Confucius to describe a man of perfection.
Confucius said: “A man of perfection must have the knowledge of Zhang Wuzhong, the freedom from greed of Gong Chao, the bravery of Bian Zhuangzi, and the varied talents of Ran Qiu, as well as the accomplishments of propriety and music.”
Then Confucius added: “Today, we do not need all of the above qualifications. When a man sees an advantage, he still thinks first if it is right for him to take. When he is in danger, he still goes ahead and does whatever he thinks is right and be willing to give up his life if necessary. He keeps his words no matter how long he made the promise. Such a man may also be called a man of perfection.”

子曰:“孟公绰为赵、魏老则优,不可以为滕、薛大夫。”

孔子说:“孟公绰可以适合做赵或魏两家的家臣,可他不宜做滕或薛两小国的大夫。”

Confucius said: “Meng Gongchao is fit to be an administrator of the noble families of Zhao or Wei, but he is not fit to be a high official of the small nations of either Teng or Xue.”

子曰:“臧武仲以防求为后于鲁,虽曰不要君,吾不信也。”

孔子说:“臧武仲以占据防邑为由,要求鲁君替他在鲁国立个后代。这个行动,虽说不是挟制,我是不相信的。”

Confucius said: “Zang Wuzhong, holding an important military town, Fang, asked the Duke of Lu to appoint a successor to him from his family. Although it may be said that he did not use force with his prince, I would not agree.”

子曰:“晋文公谲而不正,齐桓公正而不谲。”

孔子说:“晋文公狡猾而不正直。齐桓公正直而不狡猾。”

Confucius said: “The Duke Wen of Jin was crafty, but not upright, while the Duke Huan of Qi was upright, but not crafty.”

公叔文子之臣大夫僎,与文子同升诸公。子闻之曰:“可以为‘文’矣。”

公叔文子的家臣大夫僎很能干,公叔文子推荐他入朝为官与他同僚。
孔子听了后赞美说:“公叔文子真的可以称为‘文’了。”

Gong Shu Wenzi recommended his capable family officer, Zuan, to be a senior government official and went to the court with him as his colleague.
When Confucius heard of the story, he said: “Gong Shu Wenzi deserved to be given the title of ‘WEN’ (the accomplished).”

子贡曰:“管仲非仁者与?桓公杀公子纠,不能死,又相之。”
子曰:“管仲相桓公,霸诸侯,一匡天下,民到于今受其赐。微管仲,吾其被发左衽矣。岂若匹夫匹妇之为谅也,自经于沟渎,而莫之知也。”

子贡对孔子说:“管仲不是一个仁者吧?当桓公杀了公子纠后,他不能为公子纠死,反而去辅助桓公。”
孔子说:“管仲帮助桓公使其做诸侯的领袖,统一了中国,人民到今天还受到他的恩惠呢。如果没有管仲,我们早已成为野蛮人了。他岂是那班没有见识的一般男女,为了一些小信小节,自杀在水沟里也没有人知道他们的姓名。”

Zi Gong said to his master, Confucius: “Wasn't Guan Zhong a man of virtue? When the Duke Huan caused his brother, Jiu, to be killed, Guan Zhong did not die with his master, Jiu. Instead, he worked for the Duke Huan.”
Confucius said: “Guan Zhong worked for the Duke Huan as prime minister. He made the Duke Huan the leader of all the princes and rectified the whole kingdom. Even today, we still all enjoy Guan Zhong's achievements. Without Guan Zhong, we would all live like savages. He was not like some common men and women who committed suicide in the small river for frivolous matters with nobody knowing them.”

子言卫灵公之无道也。康子曰:“夫如是,奚而不丧?”
孔子曰:“仲叔圉治宾客,祝鮀治宗庙,王孙贾治军旅。夫如是,奚其丧?”

当孔子在说卫灵公的无道时,康子问:“既是如此无道,为什么他的国家还没有亡呢?”
孔子说:“因为有仲叔圉负责接待宾客,祝鮀负责宗庙事宜,王孙贾负责军事。有如此好的安排,怎么会亡国?”

When Confucius spoke about the scandalous life of the Duke Ling of Wei, Kang Zi asked: “Since the duke was of such character, how could it happen that he never lost his throne?”
Confucius answered: “He appointed Zhong Shuyu to be in charge of the affairs of receiving guests. Zhu Tuo was in charge of the ancestral temple affairs and Wang Sunjia was in charge of the military affairs. With three capable officials to be in charge of three different departments, how could the duke lose his throne?”

陈成子弑简公。孔子沐浴而朝，告于哀公曰："陈恒弑其君，请讨之。"
公曰："告夫三子。"
孔子曰："以吾从大夫之后，不敢不告也。君曰：'告夫三子者。'"
之三子告，不可。
孔子曰："以吾从大夫之后，不敢不告也。"

陈成子杀了他的国君简公。孔子沐浴后上朝，告诉哀公说："陈恒杀了他的国君，请派兵去讨伐。"
哀公说："去告诉三位大夫。"
退朝后，孔子自言自语说："因为我也在朝廷服务，所以我不能不把这件事向国君报告。现在国君说：'报告三位大夫。'"
于是，孔子去报告三位大夫。三位大夫不同意讨伐。
孔子自语道："因为我在朝廷服务，不能不把这事报告他们。"

Chen Chengzi murdered his prince, the Duke Jian of Qi. Confucius bathed first, then went to the court to report the incident to the Duke Ai: "Chen Chengzi of our neighboring state has murdered his prince. I beg Your Highness to take a military action to punish him."
Duke Ai answered: "Go tell our three ministers."
Confucius left, saying to himself: "As I am in the state council, I had to bring this matter to our prince's attention, and he said: " 'Tell our three ministers.' "
Confucius went to tell the three ministers. However, they did not agree to take military action.
Confucius said to himself: "As I am in the state council, I must bring this matter to their attention."

子路问事君。
子曰:“勿欺也,而犯之。”

子路问孔子如何去事奉国君。
孔子说:“不要欺骗他。去进谏的时候,要据理力争,不要怕会冲犯他。”

Zi Lu asked Confucius how to serve the prince.
Confucius said: “Don’t cheat him. If he makes a mistake, tell him. And don’t be afraid of offending him.”

子曰:“上好礼,则民易使也。”

孔子说:“如在上位的人喜欢遵照礼仪办事,人民便会容易使唤了。”

Confucius said: “Whenever the ruler loves to observe the rules of propriety, the people will respond readily to the calls for service.”

# 命运

公伯寮愬子路于季孙. 子服景伯以告, 曰: “夫子固有惑志于公伯寮, 吾力犹能肆诸市朝。”
子曰: “道之将行也与, 命也。道之将废也与, 命也。公伯寮其如命何?”

公伯寮在季孙面前说子路的坏话, 子服景伯告诉孔子, 说: “季孙被公伯寮所惑对子路有了怀疑, 可我仍有力量把公伯寮杀了, 并把他的尸体陈列在街上。”
孔子说: “我的大道之是否可行是命运安排的。大道是否应废也是由上天所安排的。公伯寮能违抗天命吗?”

Gong Boliao slandered Zi Lu to Ji Sun (a noble). Zifu Jingbo informed Confucius of the news, saying: “Our Master (Ji Sun) is being led astray by Gong Boliao; but I have the influence to order that man to be killed.” Confucius said: “Whether my principles can be carried out, it depends on the Heaven. If my principles can not be carried out, it also depends on the Heaven. What can Gong Boliao do against the Heaven?”

卫灵公问陈于孔子。
孔子对曰:“俎豆之事,则尝闻之矣。
军旅之事,未之学也。”
明日遂行。

卫灵公问孔子行军布阵的方法。
孔子回答:“我曾经学过宗庙祭祀的事务,
可我不知道军旅的事情。”
第二天,孔子就离开了卫国。

The Duke Ling of Wei asked Confucius about military tactics.
Confucius said: “I have learned about the rules of sacrificial affairs, but I have never learned about the military matters.”
The next day, Confucius left Wei.

子曰:“无为而治者,其舜也与。夫何为哉?
恭己正南面而已矣。”

孔子说:“以无政府的政策去治理国家可能只有舜帝吧。他做了什么?不过是恭敬地端正他的帝王品德而已。”

Confucius said: “The ancient Emperor Shun was probably the only ruler who ruled the country with a policy of no-government. What did he do? He merely behaved himself in the position he held as a ruler.”

颜渊问为邦。
子曰:"行夏之时,乘殷之辂,服周之冕,乐则韶舞。放郑声,远佞人。郑声淫,佞人殆。"

颜渊问孔子如何治国。
孔子说:"用夏代的历法,用商代的车子,穿戴周代的冕服,音乐用韶舞,不用郑国的音乐,远离搬弄是非的小人。郑国的音乐是放荡的。搬弄是非的小人是危险分子。"

Yan Yuan asked how to administrate a government.
Confucius said: "Use the calendar of the Xia dynasty; use the carriage of the Yin dynasty; wear the uniform of the present Zhou dynasty; play the music of Shao with its pantomimes; banish the songs of Zhen; and keep away from deceptive talkers. The songs of Zhen are licentious, and deceptive talkers are dangerous."

子曰:"臧文仲其窃位者与,知柳下惠之贤,而不与立也。"

孔子说:"臧文仲不是一个好官员。他明知道柳下惠有贤德,却不荐举柳与他同朝为官。"

Confucius said: " Zang Wenzhong can not be called a good official. He knew the virtue and abilities of Liu Xiahui, but he did not recommend Liu to work with him in the court."

子曰:"事君敬其事,而后其食。"

孔子说:"事奉国君,应先尽忠职守,而不要把薪金的问题过分重视。"

Confucius said: "In serving his prince, a man must do his duty faithfully first and should not be overly concerned with his salary."

季氏将伐颛臾，冉有、季路见于孔子曰："季氏将有事於颛臾。"

孔子曰："求，无乃尔是过与？夫颛臾，昔者，先王以为东蒙主，且在邦域之中矣，是社稷之臣也，何以伐为？"

冉有曰："夫子欲之。吾二臣者，皆不欲也。"

孔子曰："求，周任有言曰：'陈力就列，不能者止。'危而不持，颠而不扶，则将焉用彼相矣？且尔言过矣，虎兕出于柙，龟玉毁于椟中，是谁之过与？"

冉有曰："今夫颛臾，固而近于费，今不取，后世必为子孙忧。"

孔子曰："求，君子疾夫舍曰欲之而必为之辞。丘也闻：有国有家者，不患寡，而患不均。不患贫，而患不安。盖均无贫，和无寡，安无倾。夫如是，故远人不服，则修文德以来之。既来之，则安之。今由与求也，相夫子，远人不服，而不能来也。邦分崩离析而不能守也，而谋动干戈于邦内。吾恐季孙之忧，不在颛臾，而在萧墙之内也。"

季氏将攻打鲁国的附庸小国颛臾。冉有与季路一同来看孔子，说：'季氏将对颛臾采取军事行动。"

孔子说："冉有啊，这可能是你的过错了。那颛臾，从前是周先王封他做东蒙山主祭人的，而且在鲁国所管辖的境内，是鲁国自家的臣子啊。为什么去攻击他呢？"

冉有说："这是季氏的意思，我们两个家臣都不愿意。"

孔子说："冉有，古时的史官周任曾经说过：'如能够坚持主张，就停留在位子上，否则便应辞去。'譬如引导一个瞎子，到了危险的地方不去拉住他，跌倒地上不去扶起他，那又何必要这个引导人呢？而且你说攻打颛臾是季氏的主张，这话就更错了。譬如猛虎野牛从栏杆里冲出来，或珍贵的龟骨玉器在柜子里毁坏了，要说这不是管理人的过错，又是谁的过错？"

冉有说："如今的颛臾，城郭坚固，又接近季氏的私邑费地，如今日不取，必为后世子孙的祸害。"

孔子说："冉有，君子最痛恨的是有意避谈自己的贪得，还一定要说出一些牵强的理由。我曾经听说过：有国有家的人，不应该忧虑收入的太少，只应该顾虑不能使财富平均。不担心贫困，只担心社会不安宁。因为财富平均了，就不会产生贫困;一片和睦，就不会有人民稀少的现象;安定了就不会有覆灭的危险。果如此，如果远方的人仍不服从，在上位的人便应该修行自己的德性去感化他们，使他们来归化。来归化了，就要尽力去保护他们，使他们安定。如今，冉有和季路你们两个人辅助季氏，远方的人不服从，又没有办法使他们来归化，而本国的土地又是支离破碎，不能改善，还想要在国境内制造战争。因此，我恐怕季氏的祸患不在外面的颛臾，而在你们自己的朝中。"

The chief of a powerful noble family, Ji Shi, in the state of Lu was preparing to attack Cuan Yu, a small principality within Lu. Ran You and Ji Lu, who worked for Ji Shi, told their master, Confucius, the news.

Confucius said to Ran You: "Ran You, could it be your fault? The ruler of Cuan Yu used to preside over the sacrifices to the eastern Mong, appointed by the ancient emperor of Zhou Dynasty, and it is located within the state of Lu, thus its ruler is also a minister in direct connection with Lu. There is no reason for your chief to attack Cuan Yu."

Ran You said: "It is our chief who wants to attack Cuan Yu. We two do not want it."

Confucius said: "Zhou Ren, an ancient historian, said, 'When a man can stand the fight, he should stay in office; otherwise, he should retire.' For example, a guide tries to help a blind person. When the blind person walks to a dangerous place and the guide does not stop him, or when the blind person falls and the guide does not help him, what do we need the guide for? So your explanations are wrong. When a wild tiger or buffalo escapes from the cage, or when a tortoise shell or a piece of jade is injured in its repository, if it is not the responsibily of the person who is supposed to take care of these affairs, whose fault is it?"

Ran You said: "Today, Cuan Yu is strong and near to Fei(Ji Shi's private town). If our chief does not take it, it will be a sorrow to his descendants."

Confucius said: "Ran You, a superior man hates people who have an excuse when they ought to say simply that they want something. I have heard that the people who have a nation and a home should not worry about not having enough possessions. They should instead worry about possessions not to be evenly distributed. They should not worry about poverty, but they should worry about the lack of safety. If possessions were equally distributed, there would not be poverty. If there were mutual good will, the population would not be scarce. If people lived peacefully, there would not be fearful of the danger of loss. If all of these could be done and the faraway people still did not submit, the ruler must improve the culture and virtue to attract them to come. Once they come, the ruler must try to protect them to make them live peacefully. But now, you two, Ran You and Ji Lu, assist your master and the people faraway are not submissive, so they do not come. Meanwhile, there are divisions and downfalls in the nation, but you can not improve the situation and instead plan to create war in the nation. Therefore, I am afraid that your chief's worry is not about Cuan Yu, but it is something within his own court."

子曰:“天下有道,则礼乐征伐自天子出。天下无道,则礼乐征伐自诸侯出。自诸侯出,盖十世希不失矣。自大夫出,五世希不失矣。陪臣执国命,三世希不失矣。天下有道,则庶民不议。”

孔子说:“如果政治清明时,则礼乐的制度与征伐的号令都会出自天子之手。如果政治不清明时,礼乐的制度和征伐的号令都将出自诸侯之手。出自诸侯之手,大概十代以后很少不会丧失权势的。如果是出自大夫之手,则很少能保持到五代不会丧失权势的。如果大夫的家臣掌权了,则很少能保持到三代不会丧失权势的。当天下太平了,老百姓就不会干预国家大事了。”

Confucius said: “In a normal state of government with justice and order, the ceremonies, the music, and the military expeditions all proceed from the emperor. In an abnormal state of government without justice and order, the ceremonies, the music, and the military expeditions proceed from the princes. When these important things proceed from the princes, there are few princes who would not lose their power after ten generations. If these important things proceed from the hands of ministers, there are few ministers who would not lose their power after five generations. If these important things proceed from the hands of officers, there are few officers who would not lose their power after three generations. When there is justice and order, the common people will not meddle with the government affairs.”

子曰:“禄之去公室五世矣。政逮于大夫四世矣。故夫三桓之子孙微矣。”

孔子说:“政权不在诸侯手中已经五代了。大权被大夫抓去已经四代了。所以那桓公的后代三家大夫的子孙已经衰微了。”

Confucius said: “It has been five generations since the power of governing the nation was taken away from the princes. It has been four generations since the power of governing the nation was passed into the hands of the ruling class of ministers. Therefore, the descendants of three ruling class of ministers of the Duke Huan are now living in obscurity.”

子曰:“齐景公有马千驷,死之日,民无德而称焉。伯夷、叔齐饿于首阳之下,民到于今称之。”

孔子说:“当初齐景公有马千匹,可等到他死的时候,老百姓竟发现他没有任何功德可以称颂的。当年伯夷和叔齐一同饿死在首阳山下,一直到今天,人民还在称颂他们的仁德。”

Confucius Said: “The Duke Jing of Qi had a thousand teams of horses, yet when he died, people could not find one word to praise his virtue. The ancient worthies Bo Yi and Shu Qi starved to death at the foot of Shou Yang Mountain many years ago. People still praise their virtues today.”

子曰:"鄙夫可与事君也与哉?其未得之也,患得之。既得之,患失之。苟患失之,无所不至矣。"

孔子说:"卑鄙的人可以事奉国君吗?在没有得到职位以前,就怕得不到。得到了以后,就怕把职位丢了。因为怕丢了,什么事情都会做得出来。"

Confucius said: " How could the inferior men serve the prince? Before getting positions in the government, they were afraid of not getting them. After getting positions in the government, they were afraid of losing them. Since they were afraid of losing the positions, they would do anything they could in order to keep the positions."

子夏曰:"君子信而后劳其民。未信,则以为厉己也。信而后谏,未信,则以为谤己也。"

子夏说:"君子要先取得人民的信任,然后才可以去差使他们。如果没有取得信任,人民就会认为是虐待他们。对于国君,也要先行取得信任,然后进谏,否则国君便以为是专门找他的毛病。"

Zi Xia said: " A superior man must obtain his people's confidence first. Then he can put them to work; otherwise, people will think he is oppressing them. As for how to serve prince, he must obtain his prince's confidence first. Then he can dare to correct the prince's mistakes; otherwise, the prince will think the man only desires to find his faults."

逸民:伯夷,叔齐,虞仲,夷逸,朱张,柳下惠,少连。子曰:"不降其志,不辱其身,伯夷,叔齐与。谓柳下惠,少连,降志辱身矣,言中伦,行中虑,其斯而已矣。谓虞仲,夷逸,隐居放言,身中清,废中权。我则异于是,无可无不可。"

古时的隐士有伯夷、叔齐、虞仲、夷逸、朱张、柳下惠、少连等七人。

孔子说:"不肯丧失自己的志气,不肯辱没自己的身子,就是伯夷和叔齐这两个人了。柳下惠和少连两个人丧失了志气,辱没了身子去做官,可是他们说出来的话语还是合理的,做出来的事也不离谱,这两点还是可取的。虞仲和夷逸两个人隐藏他们的身子,故意放肆他们的言语,不过他们的隐居,尚能保守着清净的节操,所放肆的言论,尚能见机权变。我是与他们不同的。我没有哪样是绝对可以的,也没有哪样是绝对不可以的。"

In judging the worthies in the history who withdrew themselves from the world, Bo Yi, Shu Qi, Yu Zhong, Yi Yi, Zhu Zhang, Liu Xiahui, and Shao Lian, Confucius said: "Bo Yi and Shu Qi refused to decrease their will and did not want to hurt their conduct. Liu Xiahui and Shao Lian decreased their will and hurt their conduct to work for the government, but their words still corresponded with reason, and their actions were still commendable. Yu Zhong and Yi Yi secluded themselves, refusing to hold communication with the world. They succeeded in preserving purity and rightly used their discretion. As for me, I am different from those men. I have no course for which I am predetermined and no course against which I am predetermined."

孟氏使阳肤为士师，问于曾子。
曾子曰：“上失其道，民散久矣。如得其情，则哀矜而勿喜。”

孟氏派曾子的弟子阳肤为法官。阳肤向曾子请教。
曾子说：“在上位的失去正道已经很久了，所以民心早已离散了。因此，如果你发现有人犯法了，要有哀怜之心而不要沾沾自喜。”

The chief of the Meng family appointed Yang Fu, Zeng Zi's student, as the criminal judge. Yang Fu came to see Zeng Zi asking for advice.
Zeng Zi said: “Rulers have failed in their duties for a long time, and thus people have long lived in a state of disorganization. Therefore, when you find the evidence to convict a man, feel pity and be merciful to him. Do not be pleased with your findings.”

子贡曰：“纣之不善，不如是之甚也，是以君子恶居下流，天下之恶皆归焉。”

子贡说：“纣王的不善，应该不是如传说的那么厉害。所以君子不喜欢居于恶名密集的下流，因为如此一来，所有的恶事都会归结到他的头上的。”

Zi Gong said: “Former Ruler Zhou's wickedness was not as bad as what the people had said. Therefore, a superior man hates to be put in a low-lying situation, where all the evils of the world flow in upon him.”

子贡曰:“君子之过也,如日月之食焉。过也,人皆见之;更也,人皆仰之。”

子贡说:“君子的过错就好像是日蚀月蚀一样。一旦发生,大家都看见。等到改过了,人民又都可以仰望到。”

Zi Gong said: “The faults of a superior man are like the eclipses of the sun and the moon. When he does something wrong, all people will see it. Once he corrects it, all people will see it with respect, too.”

子张问于孔子曰:“何如斯可以从政矣?”
子曰:“尊五美,屏四恶,斯可以从政矣。”
子张曰:“何谓五美?”
子曰:“君子惠而不费,劳而不怨,欲而不贪,泰而不骄,威而不猛。”
子张曰:“何谓惠而不费?”
子曰:“因民之所利而利之,斯不亦惠而不费乎?择可劳而劳之,又谁怨?欲仁而得仁,又焉贪?君子无众寡,无小大,无敢慢,斯不亦泰而不骄乎?君子正其衣冠,尊其瞻视,俨然,人望而畏之,斯不亦威而不猛乎?”
子张曰:“何谓四恶?”
子曰:“不教而杀谓之虐,不戒视成谓之暴,慢令致期谓之贼,犹之与人也,出内之吝谓之有司。”

子张问孔子:"怎么样才可以从政呢?"
孔子说:"必须遵守五种美德,摒弃四种恶事,才可以从政。"
子张问:"哪五种美德?"
孔子说:"君子惠而不费,劳而不怨,欲而不贪,泰而不骄,威而不猛。"
子张问:"什么叫做惠而不费?"
孔子说:"人民认为有利的事情,当政的就让他们去做。这不就是惠而不费吗?选择可以劳动的人民去做劳动工作,又有谁会埋怨呢?实行仁政提高人民生活水准,没有人会被批评为贪得的。当一个君子处理政务时,无论对少数人或多数人,大事或小事,他都不怠慢任何一个人。这不就叫做泰而不骄吗?君子端正衣冠,态度庄严,使人民一望而生畏敬。这不就叫做威而不猛吗?"
子张问:"什么是四种恶事?"
孔子说:"不先去教导便去诛杀叫做虐;不给人民充分的时间就叫人民完成一件工程叫做暴;突然命令人民去做一项工程如不做好便予重罚叫做贼;应该付给却又不舍得叫做有司。"

Zi Zhang asked Confucius: "How could a superior man conduct the government affairs?"
Confucius said: "Five good things must be done, and four bad things must not be done."
Zi Zhang asked: "Which five good things?"
Confucius said: "Benefit the people without great expenditure, make the people labor for the public without complaint, improve the people's living conditions without being covetous, be dignified but not proud, be majestic but not fierce."
Zi Zhang asked: "How to benefit the people without great expenditure?"
Confucius said: "Let the people do the things which are beneficial to them. Isn't that to benefit the people without great expenditure? Choose the people who are capable of labor do the laboring. Who would complain? Conduct the beneficent government affairs to raise the people's living conditions. Nobody will be accused of covetousness. When a superior man deals withpeople, no matter many people, or only a few people, on important matter or unimportant matter, he never neglects any one. Isn't that to be dignified, but not proud? Being a superior man, he always dresses himself properly and acts properly. He wins people's respect. Isn't that to be majestic, but not fierce?"
Zi Zhang then asked: "Which four bad things?"
Confucius said: "Killing people without educating them first is called cruelty. Demanding people to finish a public task without giving them enough time to prepare is called oppression. Ordering people to do a project suddenly, and punishing them if it is not done well, is called injury. The payments should be made, but the payer is reluctant to do it. It is called stinginess."

# 第三章
# CHAPTER THREE

## 孔子，一位伟大的教师
## CONFUCIUS, A GREAT TEACHER

子曰:“学而时习之,不亦说乎?”

孔子说:“学习了又时常去温习,不是一件快乐的事情吗?”

Confucius said: “Isn’t it a pleasure to acquire knowledge and often review it?”

子曰:“吾与回言终日,不违如愚。退而省其私,亦足以发。回也不愚。”

孔子说:“我与颜回讲了一整天,可他都在听着而没有一句反问,就好像是个愚呆之人,没有发挥。等到他退出去了,我再观察他的生活举动,发现他把我教导他的全发挥在他的生活上了。颜回真是一点儿也不愚呆。”

Confucius said: “I have talked with Hui (a disciple) for a whole day and he never made an objection. It seemed that he was stupid, without any reaction. After schooling, I inspected his private activities and found that he did use all of my teachings in his private life. Hui is not stupid at all.”

子禽问于子贡曰:“夫子至于是邦也,必闻其政。求之与抑与之与?”
子贡曰:“夫子温、良、恭、俭、让,以得之。夫子之求之也,其诸异乎人之求之与。”

子禽问子贡:“老师每到一个国家,他必将参与那个国家的政务。这是他求得来的,还是人家请他参与的?”
子贡说:“因为老师有温和、善良、恭敬、俭约、谦逊等五种美德,因而自然地获得参与当地国家政务的机会。老师的这种获得参与与其他人等的获得参与是不同的。”

Zi Qin asked Zi Gong: “Whenever our master came to a nation, he always got involved with the politics. Did he ask for it, or was he asked for? ”
Zi Gong answered: “Our master is kind, nice, respectful, thrifty and courteous; therefore, he got involved with the politics. The way he got involved is different from the way other people got involved.”

子贡曰:“贫而无谄,富而无骄,何如?”
子曰:“可也,未若贫而乐道富而好礼者也。”
子贡曰:“诗云:‘如切如磋,如琢如磨。’其斯之谓与?”
子曰:“赐也,始可与言诗已矣,告诸往而知来者。”

子贡问孔子:“如果一个人虽然贫穷,然不谄媚;虽然富贵,然不骄傲。你觉得这个人怎么样?”
孔子说:“可以啊。可还是不如虽然贫穷仍能知足常乐、虽然富贵仍喜好礼节的更好。”
子贡说:“《诗经》说,‘如同治骨角的,切开了再去锉光;又如同治玉石的,雕琢了再去磨细’,就是这个意思吧?”
孔子说:“子贡啊,你真是一个可以和我谈诗的人,我只要告诉你一点,你就可以知道其他的部分。”

Zi Gong asked: “How do you judge the person who, though poor, does not flatter; though rich, is not proud? ”
Confucius answered: “He is all right, but it would be better if he, though poor, is still cheerful or, though rich, is still courteous.”
Zi Gong said: “I understand now. *The Book of Poetry* said, ‘After cutting, we file; after carving, we polish.’ Is that what you mean? ”
Confucius replied: “With a student like you, I can now talk about poetry. As I teach you one thing, you can apply it to others immediately.”

子曰:“视其所以,观其所由,察其所安,人焉廋哉?人焉廋哉?”

孔子说:“先看这个人所做的事情,再观察他为什么要如此做,以及他所最喜欢做的是什么,如此这个人的好好坏坏还怎么可以隐藏呢?还怎么可以隐藏呢?”

Confucius said: “If you look at a man’s doing things, then study the reason why he did it, and observe what he likes most, you will know what type of man he is. Then, how can he hide himself? how can he hide himself? ”

子曰:“温故而知新,可以为师矣。”

孔子说:“如这个人能够不断温习曾经学过的,同时再不断去学习新的知识,这个人就可以做个老师了。”

Confucius said: “ Constantly reviewing what has been acquired, and continuing to acquire new knowledge, one may thus become a teacher.”

子曰:"君子不器。"

孔子说:"君子不能像一个器皿一样,只有一种用途。"

Confucius said: "A superior man can not be like a utensil, which can be used for only one purpose."

子曰:"由,诲女知之乎?知之为知之,不知为不知,是知也。"

孔子对子路说:"我教导你的,你都知道吗?知道就是知道,不知道就是不知道。这就叫做知道。"

Confucius said to his disciple, You: "Do you understand what I taught you? If you understand it, that means you understand. If you don't understand it, that means you don't. This is called understanding."

子张学干禄。
子曰："多闻阙疑，慎言其余，则寡尤。多见阙殆，慎行其余，则寡悔。言寡尤，行寡悔，禄在其中矣。"

子张问孔子如何去得到官位。
孔子说："多去听别人说的，把怀疑的放在一边，不怀疑的部分也要谨慎地研究后再去说，如此便会很少遭到责难。多去观察别人做的，把那些使你心中不安的抛弃，对于其余的部分也要谨慎地研究后再去做，如此你就不会后悔了。如果你的言语不会被责难，行为不会后悔，自然地就会有人推荐你去做官了。"

Zi Zhang wanted to learn how to get employed in the government.
Confucius said: "Listen to the others and put aside your doubts. Even the things for which you have no doubt, you must still speak with caution. In doing these, you will not get criticized. Watch what the others do, and don't do the things about which you have doubts. Although you have no doubt about some things, you must still proceed with caution. If you follow this advice, you will not be regretful. If your speaking will not get criticized, and your doing things will not make you regretful, you will be recommended to have a position in the government."

林放问礼之本。
子曰:"大哉问!礼,与其奢也,宁俭。丧,与其易也,宁戚。"

林放问孔子什么是礼的根本。
孔子说:"这个问题真是问得好。说到礼,与其奢华浪费,不如俭约些好。参加丧礼时,与其注重表面的悲伤,不如表达内心的深度哀戚。"

Lin Fang, a Confucius' disciple, asked his master what constituted the fundamentals of propriety. Confucius answered: "That is a good question. Speaking of propriety, it is better to be frugal than extravagant. At a funeral, it is better to be deeply sorrowful in heart than to be sorrowful only for a matter of course."

子入太庙,每事问。
或曰:“孰谓鄹人之子知礼乎?入太庙,每事问。”
子闻之,曰:“是礼也。”

孔子入太庙时,遇到每一件不懂的事情都要问个明白。
有人说:“谁说那个鄹邑人的儿子懂礼仪?他进入太庙后每一件事情都要问。”
孔子听了后,说:“这就叫做礼啊。”

After Confucius entered the State Cathedral, he inquired about everything he saw.
Somebody said: “Who said the son of a man in Zou knew the rules of propriety? After he entered into the State Cathedral, he inquired about everything.”
Confucius heard this, saying: “It is called propriety.”

子曰:“参乎,吾道一以贯之。”
曾子曰:“唯。”
子出,门人问曰:“何谓也?”
曾子曰:“夫子之道,忠恕而已矣。”

孔子说:“参啊,我的道理是以一理贯通万事万物的。”
曾子说:“是的。”
孔子走出去后,别的弟子们问曾子:“这话怎么讲呢?”
曾子说:“老师的道理就是忠和恕两个字而已。”

Confucius said to his disciple, Zeng Zi, “My doctrine is an all-pervading principle.”
Zeng Zi replied, “Yes.”
Then Confucius left. His other disciples asked Zeng Zi: “What did master mean?”
Zeng Zi answered: “Our master's doctrine is comprised of only two words: faithfulness and charity.”

宰予昼寝。
子曰:“朽木不可雕也,粪土之墙,不可杇也。于予与何诛。”
子曰:“始吾于人也,听其言而信其行。今吾与人也,听其言而观其行。于予与改是。”

宰予有一天在白昼睡觉,孔子看了非常生气。
孔子说:“这真是像腐烂的木头不能用来雕刻,又好像污秽的墙壁不能粉饰。我不想去责备像宰予这样的人了。”
接着孔子又说:“从前我对于人的态度是听了他说的话,我就会相信他的行为。如今我对于人的态度则是听了他说的话后,还要去观察他的行为。这个改变是从宰予开始的。”

Confucius' disciple, Zai Yu, slept in the daytime which made Confucius angry.
Confucius scolded: “A rotten wood can not be carved. A wall built with rubbish can not be painted. I do not want to criticize a person such as Zai Yu.”
Then he added: “In the past, I liked to judge a person based on what he said, and I could predict his conduct. Now I judge a person differently. After hearing his words, I must watch his actions. I learned this change from Zai Yu.”

哀公问弟子孰为好学。
孔子对曰:“有颜回者好学,不迁怒,不贰过。不幸短命死矣。今也则亡,未闻好学者也。”

哀公问孔子弟子中谁最好学。
孔子回答:“有个学生名字叫颜回的最好学了。他从不把愤怒迁移到别人的身上,他不犯同样的错误。可惜他短命死了。现在未听说有像颜回那样好学的人。”

Duke Ai, the reigning prince of Confucius' native state, asked Confucius who, among all his disciples, was the one who most loved to learn.
Confucius answered: “There was a disciple, Yan Hui, who most loved to learn. He never transferred his anger to others. He never made the same mistake twice. Unfortunately, he did not live long and died early. Now I have not seen another who loves to learn as eagerly as did Yan Hui.”

子曰:“吾未见刚者。”
或对曰:“申枨。”
子曰:“枨也欲,焉得刚?”

孔子说:“我从未见过个性刚直的人。”
有人说:“申枨是个个性刚直的人。”
孔子说:“申枨这个人多嗜欲,怎么会是个性刚直的人?”

Confucius said: “I have never met a person who is a man of absolute uprightness.”
Somebody said: “Shen Cheng is a man of absolute uprightness.”
Confucius said: “Shen Cheng is a passionate man. How can he be called a man of absolute uprightness?”

颜渊季路侍。
子曰:“盍各言尔志?”
子路曰:“愿车马衣裘与朋友共,敝之而无憾。”
颜渊曰:“愿无伐善,无施劳。”
子路曰:“愿闻子之志。”
子曰:“老者安之,朋友信之,少者怀之。”

有一天,颜渊和子路侍立在孔子身旁。
孔子说:“为何不各自说一说你们的志向?”
子路说:“我愿意把我的车子、马和皮衣与朋友们共享,即使用旧了,我也没有遗憾。”
颜渊说:“我不愿夸张自己的才能,也不愿夸张自己的功劳。”
子路说:“我们也想听听老师你的志向。”
孔子说:“我愿天下年老的人都可有个安乐的晚年,朋友们以诚信相处,年少的人都可得到照顾。”

One day, Confucius' two disciples, Yan Yuan and Zi Lu, were attending to him.
Confucius said: “Why don't you tell your wishes? ”
Zi Lu said: “I would like to share my carriage, horses, and fine fur with friends and would not regret when they are worn out.”
Yan Yuan said: “I would not like to boast of my talents, and I would not like to boast of my accomplishments.”
Then Zi Lu asked Confucius: “May we hear your wishes? ”
Confucius said: “I wish all the aged people to live at home comfortably; all friends to show sincerity with each others; and all the youngsters to be treated carefully.”

子曰:“回也,其心三月不违仁,其余则日月至焉而已矣。”

孔子说:“颜回能长达三个月内不违背仁道,其余的学生则是几天或一个月而已。”

Confucius said: “Among my disciples, Yan Hui was the one who could keep virtue in his mind all the time without averting from it for three months. The others could keep the virtue for only several days to a month.”

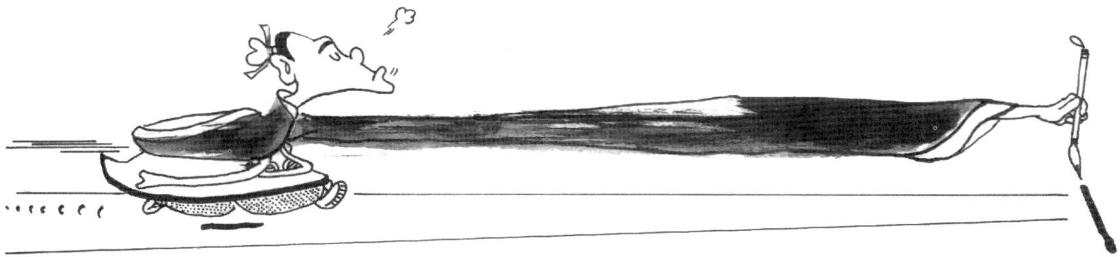

冉求曰:“非不说子之道,力不足也。”
子曰:“力不足者中道而废,今女画。”

冉求对孔子说:“我不是不喜欢你教的大道理,实在是力量不够。”
孔子说:“力量不够的人多是中途而废,如今你画一道界限,不前进了。”

Ran Qiu said to his master, Confucius: “It is not that I do not believe in your principles. It is that my strength is insufficient.”
Confucius said: “Those whose strength is insufficient give up half way. You are limiting yourself.”

子谓子夏曰:“女为君子儒,无为小人儒。”

孔子对子夏说:“你要做一个像君子样的学者,不要做一个像小人样的学者。”

Confucius said to his disciple, Zi Xia: “You should learn to be a scholar of superior man, not a scholar of inferior man.”

子曰:“孟子反不伐,奔而殿,将入门,策其马,曰:‘非敢后也,马不进也。’”

孔子说:“孟子反从不夸张他的功绩。有一次,在大退兵时,当每个人都将退入城时,他故意鞭打他的马,说:‘我并不是故意想留在大军后面殿后,实在是因为我的马跑不快啊。’”

Confucius said: “Meng Zifan never boasts of his merit. Once, when he was in the rear of a military retreat, while everybody was entering the gate, he intentionally whipped his horse, saying: ‘I would not dare to be the last one, because my horse did not advance fast.’”

子曰:“不有祝鮀之佞,而有宋朝之美,难乎免于今之世矣。”

孔子说:“如果没有像祝鮀那样的口才,宋朝那样的仪容,在现在这样的世界里是很难免除祸害的。”

Confucius said: “ Without the style of Zhu Tuo’s eloquence and the appearance of Song Chao’s handsome looks, it is hard not to escape from troubles these days.”

子曰:“谁能出不由户者?何莫由斯道也?”

孔子说:“谁能不从大门出入呢?为什么人们做事不按正道呢?”

Confucius said: “ Who can come in and go out of the house without passing through the door? Why don’t people do things based on the proper ways? ”

子曰:“知之者,不如好之者;好之者,不如乐之者。”

孔子说:“知道这道理的人,不如喜欢这道理的人;喜欢这道理的人,不如陶醉在这道理里的人。”

Confucius said: “Those who know the truth are not equal to those who love it. Those who love the truth are not equal to those who can find joy in it.”

子曰:“中人以上,可以语上也。中人以下,不可以语上也。”

孔子说:“资质在中等以上的人,可以和他谈上等的道理。资质在中等以下的人,是不能和他谈上等的道理的。”

Confucius said: “To those whose talents are above the average, the higher subjects may be discussed with them. To those whose talents are below the average, the higher subjects may not be discussed with them.”

子曰:“默而识之,学而不厌,诲人不倦,何有于我哉?”

孔子说:“默默地记住,学习永不满足,教导别人也不厌倦。这三点我做到了没有?”

Confucius said: “I put what I have seen and heard in my mind. I am fond of learning new things and never be satisfied. I like to teach other people what I have learned and I am never tired of teaching. Have I done those three things well?”

子曰:“德之不修,学之不讲,闻义不能徙,不善不能改,是吾忧也。”

孔子说:“道德不去进修,已求得的学问不去讲授,听到了义理不能遵从,有了过错不愿意去改,这些都是我所担心的。”

Confucius said: “These are my worries: not cultivating virtue, not teaching what have been learned, not moving toward what is known of righteousness, and not correcting what is wrong.”

子曰:“志于道,据于德,依于仁,游于艺。”

孔子说:“立志向道,据守德性,依从于仁,学习技艺。”

Confucius said: “Let the will be set on the path of righteousness. Let every attainment of morality be grasped. Let virtue be accorded with. Let the pursuit of arts be done smoothly.”

子曰:“自行束修以上,吾未尝无诲焉。”

孔子说:“只要有心求学,如果没钱付我正规的学费,就是送我极薄的一包肉干,我也不会不教的。”

Confucius said: “If a man wants to learn from me, even though he can not afford to pay the regular tuition fee, but bring a bundle of dried meat instead, I would never refuse to teach him.”

子曰:“不愤不启,不悱不发,举一隅不以三隅反,则不复也。”

孔子说:“如果不是他发奋要求学习,我便不去启发他。如果因为没有学习而不感到难过,我便不去启发他。如果我举一个例子,他不能推想出其他的案例,我就不想重复再说了。”

Confucius said: “If a man does not want to learn, I will not teach him. If a man does not feel regretful for he did not learn, I will not teach him. If I show a sample to the man, and he does not understand how to apply it to the other ones, I will not repeat the same lesson.”

子曰:“富而可求也,虽执鞭之士,吾亦为之;如不可求也,从吾所好。”

孔子说:“致富如果是可以求得到的,就是去做一个马夫,我也会做的。如果不是可以求得到的,我还是去做我所喜欢做的事情。”

Confucius said: “If the search for riches were able to pursue, I would do it, even if I had to be a groom with a whip in hand. If the search were not able to pursue, I would do whatever I like to do.”

子曰:“饭疏食,饮水,曲肱而枕之,乐亦在其中矣。不义而富且贵,于我如浮云。”

孔子说:“吃糙米饭,饮清水,累了便弯着手臂做枕头,乐趣就在其中。如果不是以正道去获得的富贵,对我来说,就如同天上的浮云一样。”

Confucius said: “I live on simple meals and water. When sleepy, I use my bent arm as a pillow. This is pleasure to me. If riches and honors were acquired by unrighteousness, I would see them as floating clouds in the sky.”

子曰:“加我数年,五,十以学易,可以无大过矣。”

当孔子在研究《易经》时,他说:“再有个五到十年左右,我就可以完全明了了。”

While Confucius was studying *The Book of Change*, he said: “In another five to ten years, I think I'll completely understand the book without any problems.”

子所雅言：诗，书，执礼，皆雅言也。

孔子平日所喜欢说的，不外乎是诗和历史以及要遵守礼仪等。

The subjects Confucius liked to talk about frequently were poetry, history and the rules of propriety.

子不语：怪，力，乱，神。

孔子不喜欢谈怪异、暴力、悖乱和鬼神等的题目。

Confucius does not talk these subjects: supernatural phenomena, extraordinary feats of strength, unreasonable disorder, and spiritual beings.

子曰:“吾非生而知之者,好古敏以求之也。”

孔子说:“我不是天生就知道一切事理的。我因为喜欢研究古时的历史及不断地学习才有今日的。”

Confucius said: “I am not a man who is born to know everything. I am but a man who is fond of antiquities and diligent in studying them.”

子曰:“三人行,必有我师焉。择其善者而从之,其不善者而改之。”

孔子说:“每三个人中,就必然会有一个人可以做我的老师,因为每个人必会知道一些那两个人所不知道的事情,我跟这个人去学习他的好的一面;如果这个人有不好的地方而我也有,那我就将它改掉。”

Confucius said: “Among every three people I am with, one of them will be my teacher. Everybody knows something which the other two people do not know. I learn the good parts from that person. If that person has some bad part which I also have, I will correct it.”

子曰:"二三子以我为隐乎?吾无隐乎尔。吾无行而不与二三子者,是丘也。"

孔子对他的弟子们说:"你们以为我有什么道理隐藏着不肯教导你们吗?我没有隐藏。我把我所知道的都教导给你们了。这就是我一向的作风啊。"

Confucius said: "My disciples, do you think I have concealed something of not having taught you? I conceal nothing from you. There is nothing that I have not shown to you. This is the way I do."

子以四教:文、行、忠、信。

孔子平日教导他的弟子们这下面四种科目:文化、行为、忠诚、信实。

Confucius liked to teach his disciples the following four subjects: culture, conduct, faithfulness and truthfulness.

子曰:"圣人吾不得而见之矣,得见君子者斯可矣。"

孔子说:"如果我见不到圣人,能见到君子也应该满足了。"

Confucius said: "If I do not meet a sage, I should be satisfied to see a man of virtue."

子曰:"善人吾不得而见之矣,得见有恒者斯可矣。亡而为有,虚而为盈,约而为泰,难乎有恒矣。"

孔子说:"如果我见不到真正诚恳的好人,能见到遵守常理的人也就满足了。今天,人们喜欢将没有假装为有,空虚假装充实,贫穷假装富足。这种人是很难去遵守常理的。"

Confucius said: "If I do not meet an absolutely honest man, I should be satisfied to see a man who possesses constancy. Today, people, who don't have, like to pretend they have; people, who have nothing, like to pretend they have plenty; people, who are poor, like to pretend they are rich. For these kinds of people, it is no wonder why they do not possess constancy."

子曰:“盖有不知而作之者,我无是也。多闻,择其善者而从之,多见而识之,知之次也。”

孔子说:“有一种人明明是不知道,而竟假装知道去做了。我是不会如此的。一个人应当多听别人说,然后选择那些对的去做。多看别人做,然后记在心里。这些便可以差不多是他的知识了。”

Confucius said: “There are some people who do not have knowledge, yet they pretend they have and go ahead to do it. I am not this kind of person. A person should hear as mush as he can, then select the good parts to follow ; meanwhile, he should memorize what he has seen. Those would be nearly his knowledge. ”

互乡难与言，童子见，门人惑。
子曰："与其进也，不与其退也，唯，何甚。人洁己以进，与其洁也，不保其往也。"

互乡地方的人很难和他们沟通。有一个童子从那儿来见孔子，孔子竟接见了。弟子们很不解。
孔子说："人家有礼貌而来，就不能让他退回去。不可太过分了。人家端庄地来见我，我就应当赞许，不要计较他们以往的行为。"

The people of a place called Hu Xiang were noted for being difficult to talk with. A young man from Hu Xiang came to see Confucius and Confucius received him. His disciples were confused why their master received a person from that place.
Confucius explained: "When he is polite, we should not turn down him. We should not criticize too much. If a person comes to see us in good manner, we should accept him and disregard his past."

陈司败问:“昭公知礼乎?”
孔子曰:“知礼。”
孔子退,揖巫马期而进之,曰:“吾闻君子不党,君子亦党乎?君取于吴,为同姓,谓之吴孟子。君而知礼孰不知礼?”
巫马期以告。
子曰:“丘也幸,苟有过,人必知之。”

陈司败问孔子:“昭公知道礼仪吗?”
孔子说:“知道。”
孔子退出后,陈司败把巫马期请进来,问道:“我听说君子是不偏袒的。君子也会偏袒吗?鲁君娶了同姓的吴国女子,改名叫吴孟子。你说鲁君知道礼仪还是不知道?”
事后巫马期把这话告诉了孔子。
孔子说:“我真幸运。我一旦犯错,别人就必会知道。”

Chen Sibai asked: “ Did Duke Zhao know the rules of propriety? ”
Confucius answered: “Yes.”
After Confucius left, Chen Sibai asked Wu Maqi to come in and asked: “I have heard that a superior man is not partisan. Is superior man partisan? The prince married a girl with the same family name as his and he changed the girl’s name as Wu Meng zi. Do you think the prince knew the rules of Propriety or not? ”
Later, Wu Maqi told Confucius the conversation.
Confucius said: “I am lucky. Whenever I make a mistake, people know it immediately.”

子疾病，子路请祷。
子曰:"有诸?"
子路对曰:"有之。诔曰:'祷尔于上下神祇。'"
子曰:"丘之祷久矣。"

孔子生病了。子路请求准许他代向神明祈祷保佑。
孔子说:"有这个道理吗?"
子路回答:"有的。祷文不是说过'为你祷告那天地间一切神明。'"
孔子说:"那我早已祷告过了。"

Confucius was sick. His disciple, Zi Lu, asked for permission to pray for him.
Confucius asked: "May such a thing be done?"
Zi Lu answered: "Yes, *The Book of Rituals* says, 'Pray to the spirits of the upper and lower worlds for you.'"
Confucius said: "If that's the case, I have been doing this for a long time."

子曰:“奢则不孙,俭则固。与其不孙也,宁固。”

孔子说:“太奢侈了便会超越礼仪,太节俭了便会变成简陋。与其超越礼仪,不如简陋的好。”

Confucius said: “Extravagance leads to insubordination; and parsimony leads to simplism. It is better to be simplified than to be insubordinate.”

曾子曰:“以能问于不能,以多问于寡,有若无,实若虚,犯而不校,昔者,吾友尝从事于斯矣。”

曾子说:“自己有能力,去请教没有多少能力的人;自己知识很多,去请教知识不足的人;有本事,却看来像没有本事的人;很充实,却表示出像个空虚的人;别人触犯了他,他也不计较。以前我有一个朋友曾经是个如此的人。”

Zeng Zi said: “Gifted with ability, yet seeking advice from persons who do not have much ability; possessed of much knowledge, yet seeking advice from persons who have less knowledge; rich in ability, yet appearing having no ability; profound, yet appearing empty; being offended, yet not minded. I had a friend who was such a person.”

子曰:"兴于诗,立于礼,成于乐。"

孔子说:"读诗可以启发一个人的心志,学礼可以使一个人的品格坚定,听音乐可以使一个人的心境平静。"

Confucius said: " Studying poetry can inspire a man's mind. Learning the rules of propriety can make a man's character resolute. Listening to music can make a man feel peaceful."

子曰:"好勇疾贫,乱也。人而不仁,疾之已甚,乱也。"

孔子说:"一个人如果很勇敢可又怨恨贫穷,一定会出乱子的。一个没有仁德心的人,如果你一而再不断地去责难他,他就会出乱子的。"

Confucius said: " If a man is brave, but he hates to be poor, he will most likely put the society in disorder. If a man does not have any virtue, and everybody keeps blaming him, he will also put the society in disorder."

子曰:“狂而不直,侗而不愿,悾悾而不信,吾不知之矣。”

孔子说:“狂妄又不正直,无知又不谨慎,没有任何本领而又不信实,对于这种人,我真不明了他们。”

Confucius said: “Arrogant and yet not upright, lacking knowledge and yet not being cautious, having no abilities and yet not being faithful. I do not understand these kinds of people.”

子罕言利与命与仁。

孔子很少谈到利益和命运与仁道的关系。

Confucius seldom talked about the relationship between profit and fortune as well as virtue.

子绝四:毋意,毋必,毋固,毋我。

这四种心态孔子都没有:不任意猜测,不武断,不固执己见,不自私自利。

There were four things from which Confucius was totally free: He was free from prejudgment, free from predeterminations, free from obstinacy, and free from selfishness.

子曰:“吾有知乎哉?无知也。有鄙夫问于我,空空如也,我叩其两端而竭焉。”

孔子说:“我有知识吗?也没有太多的知识。但是,假如有一个粗俗的人问我,因为他是空无一点知识,我还是会把道理从头到尾全都告诉他的。”

Confucius said: “Do I have knowledge? I don’t have much. However, if an uneducated man asks me a question, I will explain it to him from all aspects.”

子见齐衰者，冕衣裳者，与瞽者，见之，虽少必作。过之必趋。

当孔子在路上看见穿丧服的人，或穿着正式礼服的人，或盲人时，虽然这些人的年纪也许很轻，他也会站在路边让他们先走过。如果他必须要穿过这些人时，他一定加快脚步。

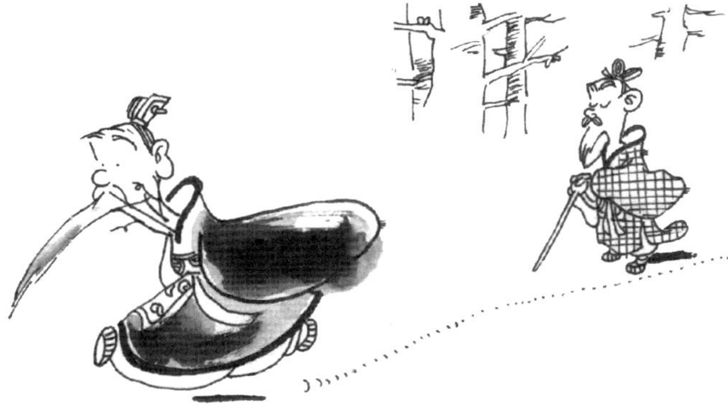

Whenever Confucius was traveling on a road and saw a person dressed in deep mourning, or in formal dress, or a blind person, although they might be young people, he would stand by the roadside to let them go first. If he had to pass them, he would do it quickly.

子曰："出则事公卿，入则事父兄，丧事不敢不勉，不为酒困，何有于我哉。"

孔子说："出外在政府服务，对公卿忠诚；到了家里，对父兄孝敬；参加丧事，尽到了哀伤；喝酒时，不为酒醉所困；我不知道我都做到了没有。"

Confucius said: "In government, serving the princes and ministers loyally; at home, serving father and elder brothers respectfully; at a funeral, performing the sorrowful duties accordingly; when drinking, not getting drunk. I don't know if I have accomplished all of these."

颜渊喟然叹曰:“仰之弥高,钻之弥坚。瞻之在前,忽焉在后。夫子循循然善诱人。博我以文,约我以礼,欲罢不能。既竭吾才,如有所立卓尔。虽欲从之,末由也矣。”

颜渊感慨地赞叹他老师孔子的学问说:“就好像愈是仰望愈觉得高深莫测,愈是钻研愈觉其坚实。有时看见好像就在前面,可是当我想抓住它时,它又忽然间转到后面。老师善于诱导,他教我各种典籍,又教我要以礼仪来约束,使我无法停下来不去学习。我已经尽了我的力了,可老师的大道仍然卓立在我的面前,我很想追上前去,可又无法追及。”

Yan Yuan, Confucius' most favorite disciple, said in admiration of his master: “The more I want to imitate my master, the more I find that it is too high an endeavor, and after studying, I find it too strong. His doctrines seem to be right in the front, but if I try to catch them, they quickly switch to the back. My master knows how to induce us to learn. He taught me all kinds of classics first, then the rules of propriety to restrict what I have learned. I can not stop learning from him and must do all my best to learn. His doctrines are still standing right there. I want to chase after them, but I just can not catch up.”

子疾病。子路使门人为臣。
病闲，曰："久矣哉由之行诈也。无臣而为有臣，吾谁欺？欺天乎？且予与其死于臣之手也，无宁死于二三子之手乎。且予纵不得大葬，予死于道路乎？"

孔子得了重病，子路准备办理丧事，要别的弟子们假装为家臣。
孔子病好后知道了这件事，他责备子路说："你做这种欺诈的事想必已是很久了，我没有家臣，而你假装我有家臣，我欺骗谁啊？欺骗老天吗？我与其死在家臣之手，还不如死在你们弟子之手的好。更何况我虽然得不到做大臣的葬礼，难道我还会死在路上没人安葬吗？"

When Confucius was very ill, his disciple, Zi Lu, was preparing an official funeral and planned to assign the other disciples to act as officers.
When Confucius got better, he scolded Zi Lu: "You must have conducted this deception for a long time. I did not have officers, but you pretended that I had. Whom should I cheat? Should I cheat Heaven? I would rather die in the hands of my disciples than in the hands of the so-called officers. Although I would not get an official funeral, neither would I die by the roadside? "

子在川上，曰："逝者如斯夫，不舍昼夜。"

孔子站在河水边，看到那不停的流水，说："天地间的事，就像流水一样地过去，日夜不停，不再回头。"

When Confucius was standing by a stream, he remarked: "All the matters are passing away just like running water day and night."

子曰："吾未见好德如好色者也。"

孔子说："我还没有见到一个男子喜欢仁德如同喜欢女色一样。"

Confucius said: "I have never seen a man who is as fond of virtue as the beauty of a woman."

子曰:“譬如为山,未成一篑,止,吾止也;譬如平地,虽覆一篑,进,吾往也。”

孔子说:“求学就如同挑土筑山一般,如果只差一筐土就可以筑成一座小山而我停下来了,那工作没有完成便是因为我停下来了;又如同把小山铲为平地一般,如果我多铲了一筐土,那就是说我仍在继续前进中。”

Confucius said: “Learning may be compared to what may happen in making a mound of earth. If there is only one bucket of earth needed to complete the work, and I stop, it means that the work is not complete because of my stopping. When I am tossing the earth onto the ground, with another bucket of earth to be thrown, it means that I am still advancing.”

子曰:“语之而不惰者,其回也与。”

孔子说:“听我的教导而不表露一点困倦的就是颜回了。”

Confucius said: “Listening without showing any tiredness while I was teaching was Yan Hui only.”

子谓颜渊曰:“惜乎,吾见其进也,未见其止也。”

谈到颜回,孔子说:“真可惜他死了,他在世时,我只看见他在学习进步,从未见他停止学习过。”

Talking about Yan Yuan, Confucius mourned: “Alas! He was dead. When he was alive, I always saw him advancing. I never saw him stop learning.”

子曰:“苗而不秀者,有矣夫;秀而不实者,有矣夫。”

孔子说:“人就像谷物一样。有的发苗而不开花,有的开花而不结果实。”

Confucius said: “People are like corns. Some only sprout up, but do not flower; and some flower, but do not ripen into fruits.”

子曰:“法语之言,能无从乎?改之为贵。巽与之言,能无说乎?绎之为贵。说而不绎,从而不改,吾未如之何也已矣。”

孔子说:“假如你正正经经地去对一个人讲话,他能不听吗?有过能改是可贵的。假如你和他好好地讲,他能不愉快吗?能去分析是可贵的。假如他只是表面愉快而并不去分析,或者虽然在听而不去改过,对于这种人,我也无能为力了。”

Confucius said: “If you speak to a man very seriously, how can he not listen to you? Correcting is the most important thing. If you speak to a man in a friendly manner, how can he not be happy ? Being able to examine is the most important thing. If a person seems happy, but he does not want to examine; or if a person is listening, but does not correct his mistake, for those people, I can do nothing.”

子曰:“三军可夺帅也,匹夫不可夺志也。”

孔子说:“统领三军的大帅有时仍可以把他抓过来,如果一个人的意志坚定了,则是无论如何也改变不了的。”

Confucius said: “The commander-in-chief of an army may be carried off, but a man’s will can not be taken away once it is firm.”

子曰:“衣敝缊袍与衣狐貉者立而不耻者,其由也与!”

孔子说:“穿着破旧的棉袍与那穿着狐皮或貉皮的人站在一起而不感到羞耻的,恐怕只有仲由了。”

Confucius said: “ Dressed in an old shabby suit made of cheap cloth, standing next to the man dressed in costly furs, without feeling ashamed, is my disciple, Zhong You!”

“不忮不求,何用不臧?”子路终身诵之。子曰:“是道也,何足以臧。”

“不起妒忌心,不起贪求心,怎么会不好呢?”子路不停地去诵读。
孔子说:“是不错的,可也不是十分完美的。”

“ Without enry, without greed, how could it not be good?” Zi Lu kept repeating these words.
Confucius said: “It is all right, but still not perfect.”

子曰:"岁寒,然后知松柏之后凋也。"

孔子说:"只有到了严冬的时候,方才知道松树和柏树是最后凋谢的。"

Confucius said: "Only when the cold winter comes, we realize that the pine tree and the cypress are the last ones to lose their green."

子曰:"可与共学,未可与适道。可与适道,未可与立。可与立,未可与权。"

孔子说:"可以和有些人共同学习,但不一定可以和他们一同奉行正道;可以和一些人一同奉行正道,但不一定可以和他们一同坚守正道;可以和一些人一同坚守正道,但不一定可以和他们一同遇事权衡轻重。"

Confucius said: " We may study with some people, but we may not share principles with them. We may share principles with them, but we may not stand firm together. We may stand firm with them, but we may not deliberate together."

季路问事鬼神。
子曰:"未能事人,焉能事鬼?"
敢问死。
曰:"未知生,焉知死?"

季路问孔子如何事奉鬼神。
孔子说:"我们事奉活的人还不够诚敬,如何可以谈到去事奉鬼神呢?"
季路又问人死后的情形。
孔子说:"我们还不知道生命的意义是什么,哪里还能谈到死后的情形?"

Ji Lu (also known as Zi Lu) asked his master how to serve the spirits of the dead.
Confucius replied: "Since we can not do well to serve the living people, how can we talk about to serve the spirits of the dead?"
Ji Lu then inquired about death.
Confucius replied: "Since we do not fully realize the meaning of life, how can we realize the meaning of death?"

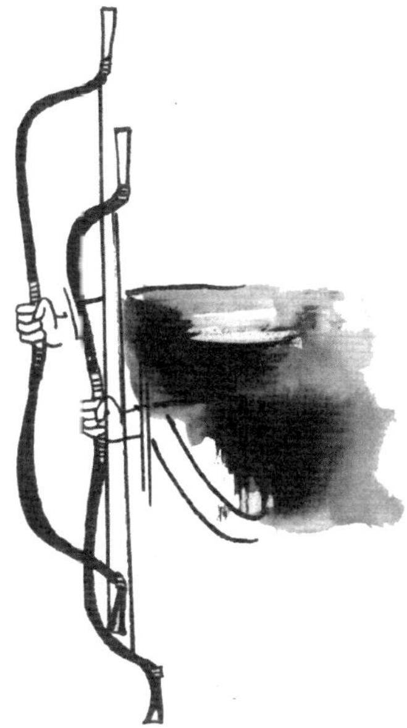

子贡问:"师与商也孰贤?"
子曰:"师也过,商也不及。"
曰:"然则师愈与?"
子曰:"过犹不及。"

子贡问孔子:"师和商两个人,哪一个比较贤明?"
孔子说:"师做事太过了点,而商则有时又不足。"
子贡说:"那是说师是比较贤明了?"
孔子说:"太过和不足的毛病是一样的。"

Zi Gong asked his master which of the two disciples, Shi and Shang, was more superior.
Confucius replied: "Shi often goes beyond the mark, while Shang often does not reach it."
Zi Gong asked again: "Do you mean Shi is more superior? "
Confucius replied again: "To go beyond is just as bad as not to reach it."

子曰:"回也其庶乎,屡空。赐不受命,而货殖焉,亿则屡中。"

孔子说:"颜回的学识几已完美了,可是他一直生活在贫困中。子贡不肯听天由命,做生意很成功,因为他对物价的猜测多是对的。"

Confucius said: "Hui is almost perfect, yet he always lives in poverty. Zi Gong does not believe in fortune. He knows how to increase his wealth as he has the ability to predict the prices of merchandise."

子张问善人之道。
子曰:"不践迹,亦不入于室。"

子张问孔子什么是善人。
孔子说:"善人是不依照别人的方式去做的,可也尚未达到仁者的境界。"

Zi Zhang asked what were the characteristics of a good man. Confucius said: " A good man does not follow the footsteps of other people; however, he is not yet a man of virtue."

子曰:“论笃是与,君子者乎,色庄者乎?”

孔子说:“如果一个人的态度看来真诚,我们是否就可以认为他是个君子呢,抑或不过是位态度庄严的人呢?”

Confucius said: “If a man’s manner appears sincere, should we call him a superior man, or just a man with a serious appearance?”

子曰:“博学于文,约之以礼,亦可以弗畔矣夫。”

孔子说:“一个人如能广博学习,一切又都安礼仪办理,他的行为就不会违背义理了。”

Confucius said: “If a man can study all the teachings, as well as follow the rules of propriety, he will not overstep what is right.”

子路问:“闻斯行诸?”
子曰:“有父兄在,如之何其闻斯行之。”
冉有问:“闻斯行诸?”
子曰:“闻斯行之。”
公西华曰:“由也问闻斯行诸,子曰:‘有父兄在。’求也问闻斯行诸,子曰:‘闻斯行之。’赤也惑。敢问?”
子曰:“求也退,故进之。由也兼人,故退之。”

子路问孔子:“当我听到一件事情,是否应该立刻去做?”
孔子说:“你的父兄仍在,如何可以立刻去做。”
冉有也问孔子:“当我听到一件事情,是否应该立刻去做?”
孔子说:“是的,你应该立刻去做。”孔子的另一个弟子公西华问孔子:“子路问你如果听到了一件事情,是否应该立刻去做,你说:‘有父兄在,如何可以。’冉有也问你如果听到一件事情,是否应该立刻去做,你回答说:‘你应该立刻做。’我可迷惑了,请告诉我为什么。”
孔子说:“冉有犹豫太过,所以我鼓励他前进。子路的资质刚强,所以我有意抑制他。”

Zi Lu asked: “Should I should carry out immediately a task which I have just heard?”
Confucius answered: “Your father and elder brother are still alive. How can you carry out immediately.”
Soon afterwards, another disciple, Ran You, asked: “Should I carry out immediately a task which I have just heard?”
Confucius answered: “Yes, you should do it immediately.”
Gong Xihua, another disciple, asked his master, “When Zi Lu asked you if he should carry out immediately a task which he had just heard and you replied, ‘Your father and elder brother are still alive. How can you carry out immediately?’ But when Ran You asked you if he should carry out immediately a task which he had just heard and you replied, ‘Yes, you should do it immediately.’ I am confused. Please tell me how.”
Confucius explained: “Ran You hesitates too much, so I encouraged him to go ahead. Zi Lu is too forward, so I wanted to hold him back a little bit.”

子张问:"士,何如斯可谓之达矣?"
子曰:"何哉尔所谓达者?"
子张对曰:"在邦必闻,在家必闻。"
子曰:"是闻也,非达也。夫达也者,质直而好义,察言而观色,虑以下人,在邦必达,在家必达。夫闻也者,色取仁而行违,居之不疑,在邦必闻,在家必闻。"

子张问孔子:"做为一个士人,如何才可以通达?"
孔子问:"你之所谓通达是什么意思?"
子张说:"在邦国里有名气,在家族里有名气。"
孔子说:"这是有名气而不是通达。所谓通达必须心地正直而好义举,从别人的脸色中可以看出自己的行为是否端正,常常想到谦恭待人。这样的人在邦国里必然通达,在家族里也必然通达。至于说有名气,有些人在表面上看来好像是仁者,实际上他是违反仁道的;自己以为不错,其实是在求名。这种人在邦国里有名气,在家族里也有名气。"

Zi Zhang asked: "What can an educated man do in order to be distinguished?"
Confucius said: "What do you mean to be distinguished?"
Zi Zhang answered: "To be well known in the nation as well as in the clan."
Confucius said: "This is to be well known, not to be distinguished. In order to be distinguished, a man must do the acts of righteousness. Frequently examining other people's words and looking at other people's countenances, he will know if he is humble enough. He always thinks how to treat others humbly. Such a man will be distinguished in the nation as well as in his clan. As for to be well known, the man may look like a person of virtue. Actually, he is not. He thinks he is doing right; actually, he is but seeking fame. Such a man will be well known in the nation as well as in his clan."

樊迟从游于舞雩之下,曰:"敢问崇德,修慝,辨惑?"
子曰:"善哉问。先事后得,非崇德与!攻其恶,无攻人之恶,非修慝与!一朝之忿,忘其身以及其亲,非惑与!"

樊迟跟随孔子休息在一座祭坛下面。他问孔子:"要怎样才可以崇扬德行、消除怨恶和辨明迷惑?"
孔子说:"问得好。如果是一件好事,就得立刻去做,当要获得什么酬劳时,走在后面,这不就是崇扬德行么!当发现错误时,他应该先责备自己,不要去责备别人,这不就是消除怨恶么!当一个人在盛怒时,往往会带来麻烦,有时还要连累父母,那不就是迷惑么!"

Accompanying his master to rest by an altar, Fan Chi asked: "May I know how to increase virtue, how to decrease hatred, and how to dismiss delusion? "
Confucius answered: "Those are good questions. When it is a right thing, go ahead to do it. When it is the time to be rewarded, stay behind. Aren't methods to increase virtue! When a person discovers a wrong thing, he should blame himself first, not others. Wouldn't this decrease hatred! When a man is furious, he often brings troubles to himself and, sometimes, his parents, too. Isn't that a delusion! "

樊迟问仁。
子曰:“爱人。”
问知。
子曰:“知人。”
樊迟未达。子曰:“举直错诸枉,能使枉者直。”
樊迟退。见子夏曰:“乡也,吾见于夫子而问知,子曰:‘举直错诸枉,能使枉者直。’何谓也?”
子夏曰:“富哉言乎。舜有天下,选于众,举皋陶,不仁者远矣。汤有天下,选于众,举伊尹,不仁者远矣。”

樊迟问孔子怎样才算是仁。
孔子说:“要能够爱人。”
樊迟又问孔子怎样才算是智。
孔子说:“要能够识出人的好坏。”
樊迟依然不明白。孔子说:“举用正直的人,除去邪恶的人,就可以使邪恶也变成正直。”
樊迟退出后,见到了子夏,说:“我曾经问老师怎样才算是智,老师说:‘举用正直的人,除去邪恶的人,就可以使邪恶变成正直。’这究竟是什么意思?”

子夏说:“回答得很有道理呀。从前舜做天子时,在众多人中挑选执法官员,最后选上了皋陶,于是那些不仁的人便远离了。等到商汤做了天子,他也在众多人中挑选执法官员,最后选上了伊尹,于是那些不仁的人便都远离了。”

Fan Chi asked what benevolence is.
Confucius said: “To love people.”
Then Fan Chi asked what wisdom is.
Confucius said: “To understand people.”
Fan Chi did not understand.
Confucius continued: “Employing the people of uprightness, putting aside the crooks, will make the crooks upright.”
Fan Chi departed, asking another disciple, Zi Xia, “I asked our master about wisdom, and he said that employing the people of uprightness and putting aside the crooks would make the crooks upright. What does that mean? ”
Zi Xia said: That's a good answer. In the early years, when Shun was the ruler of the kingdom, he chose Gao Tao to be the minister of justice among all the people and officials. Thus all the crooks disappeared. When Tang became the ruler of the kingdom, he chose Yi Yin to be the minister of justice among all the people and officials. Thus all the crooks disappeared.”

子贡问友。
子曰:"忠告而善道之,不可,则止,毋自辱焉。"

子贡问孔子如何交朋友。
孔子说:"朋友犯了过错时,要忠告他,并且要说得婉转。如果朋友不听,那就算了,不要再说了,否则便会自讨没趣的。"

Zi Gong asked about friendship.
Confucius said: " When you find that your friend has a mistake, you should advise him as faithfully and skillfully as you can. If he does not accept your advice, avoid giving him more advice. Otherwise, he will be angry with you, and you will be disgraced."

曾子曰:"君子以文会友,以友辅仁。"

曾子说:"君以学术文章去与朋友交往,因为这类朋友的交往也可以辅助仁德之增进。"

Zeng Zi said: " A superior man makes friends by the method of learning arts and literature together, as such a friendship helps practice the virtue, too."

樊迟请学稼。
子曰:“吾不如老农。”
请学为圃。
曰:吾不如老圃。”
樊迟退。
子曰:“小人哉,樊须也。上好礼,则民莫敢不敬。上好义,则民莫敢不服。上好信,则民莫敢不用情。夫如是,则四方之民襁负其子而至矣,焉用稼?”

樊迟请教孔子关于种五谷的事情。
孔子说:“关于这方面的知识,我是不如一个老农夫的。”
于是樊迟又请教孔子关于种果蔬的事情。
孔子说:“关于种果蔬方面的知识,我是不如一个老园丁的。”
等樊迟退出了以后,孔子对其他的学生们说:“樊迟这个人实在太庸俗了。如果在上位的人能够爱好礼法,人民就没有一个会不去尊敬他的;如果在上位的人能够爱好义理,人民就没有一个会不服从他的;如果在上位的能够遵守信用,人民就没有一个会不用真情去对待他的。果然如此了,则四方之人民都会背着儿女来归化的,在上位的人哪里还用得着要自己去种五谷呢?”

Fan Chi wanted to learn farming from Confucius.

Confucius said: “My knowledge about farming is not as good as a farmer's.”

Then Fan Chi wanted to learn gardening from Confucius.

Confucius said: “My knowledge about gardening is not as good as a gardener's.”

After Fan Chi left the room, Confucius said to his other disciples: “What a vulgar man Fan Chi is. If the rulers of nation did things all according to propriety, the people would not dare not to respect them. If the rulers did things all according to righteousness, the people would not dare not to obey them. If the rulers did things all according to faithfulness, the people would not dare not to be sincere with them. In this case, people from all directions will bring their families and move to this nation. Therefore, how do we need the rulers to farm themselves?”

子曰:"诵诗三百,授之以政,不达。使于四方,不能专对。虽多,亦奚以为?"

孔子说:"一个人背诵了三百篇诗以后,拿政事交给他办,如果办不好,再派他出使异国,结果也不能处理。对于这种人,读再多的诗对他又有什么用处呢?"

Confucius said: " If a man can recite three hundred pieces of poetry by heart, but he can not handle the domestic government affairs well; then send him to a foreign nation and he can not handle foreign affairs well, too, for this kind of person, what does he need for reciting more poems? "

子曰:"南人有言曰:'人而无恒,不可以作巫医。'善夫,不恒其德,或承之羞。"

孔子说:"南国的人有句话说:'如果没有恒心,是不可以做巫医的。'这话说得很对。《易经》上也说,如果一个人不能保持他良好的品德,迟早他会被羞辱的。"

Confucius said: "The people in the south have a saying, 'A man without perseverance can not become a doctor of wizard.' That is true! *The Book of Change* also says that if a man can not keep his good reputation, sooner or later, he will be disgraced."

子贡问曰:“乡人皆好之,何如?”
子曰:“未可也。”
“乡人皆恶之,何如?”
子曰:“未可也。不如乡人之善者好之,其不善者恶之。”

子贡问孔子:“如果乡里中的人都说某人是个好人,你认为如何呢?”
孔子说:“还是不能就相信他是好人的。”
子贡又问:“如果乡里中的人都说他是个坏人,你认为如何呢?”
孔子说:“也是不能就此相信的。必须乡里中的好人说他是好人,而不好的人又说他是坏人,那才是最重要的。”

Zi Gong asked: “If all the persons in the neighborhood liked a certain man, what would you think of this man? ”
Confucius said: “It would not matter.”
Zi Gong asked: “If all the persons in the neighborhood disliked him, what would you think of this man? ”
Confucius said: “It would not matter, either. If all the good persons in the neighborhood liked him, and all the bad persons in the neighborhood disliked him, that would be the most important.”

子曰:“善人教民七年,亦可以即戎矣。”

孔子说:“如果有善人来教导人民七年,人民就可以武装起来保卫国家了。”

Confucius said: “When a righteous man educates the people for seven years, the people will be effective enough to be armed to defend the nation.”

子曰:“君子而不仁者有矣夫。未有小人而仁者也。”

孔子说:“君子中有时也会有人做出不仁的事情,但从没有小人会做仁德之事的。”

Confucius said: “Among the superior men, some occasionally may do some not virtuous things; but, among the inferior men, none would do a virtuous thing.”

子曰:“爱之能勿劳乎?忠焉能勿诲乎?”

孔子说:“爱子女就能让他们不做劳动工作吗?对君主尽忠,如果他犯了错难道就不予规谏吗?”

Confucius said: “Because we love our children, can we not let them do laboring jobs? Because we are faithful to our prince, when he makes a mistake, can we not give him advice? ”

子曰:“贫而无怨,难;富而无骄,易。”

孔子说:“要贫穷的人不怨恨,是很难的。要富贵的人不骄傲,是容易的。”

Confucius said: “It is difficult for a pocr person not to complain about his poverty, while it is easy for a rich person not to be proud of his wealth.”

子问公叔文子于公明贾曰:“信乎夫子不言不笑不取乎?”
公明贾对曰:“以告者过也。夫子时然后言,人不厌其言。乐然后笑,人不厌其笑。义然后取,人不厌其取。”
子曰:“其然岂其然乎?”

孔子向公明贾询问他的老师公叔文子的做人:“人家都说你的老师不喜欢说话、不喜欢笑也不取财物,真的吗?”
公明贾说:“这是告诉你话的人言过其实了。事实上,我的老师还是喜欢说话的,不过他是在应该说的时候说话,所以人们不讨厌他说的话;他在快乐的时候笑,所以人们不讨厌他的笑。他在认为他应该取财的时候取,所以人们不讨厌他的取。”
孔子说:“他真是这样的吗?”

Confucius asked Gong Mingjia about his teacher, Gong Shu Wenzi: “Is true that your teacher seldom speaks, seldom laughs and seldom takes?”
Gong Mingjia said: “What someone told you is not completely true. My teacher speaks when it is the time to speak; therefore, people are not tired of his speaking. He laughs when he is happy; therefore, people are not tired of his laughing. He takes when it is right for him to take; therefore, people are not tired of his taking.”
Confucius said: “Is that really so?”

子曰:“骥,不称其力,称其德也。”

孔子说:“骥之所以被称为上等好马,不是因为它有跑得快的本领,而是说它有驯良的德性。”

Confucius said: “A horse may be called a fine horse because it has high moral qualities, nct because it has brute strength.”

子曰:“赐也,女以予为多学而识之者与?”
对曰:“然,非与?”
曰:“非也,予一以贯之。”

孔子对子贡说:“赐啊,你以为我真是个学识很博又能强记在心的人么?”
子贡说:“是呀,难道你不是吗?”
孔子说:“不是的,我不过是用一个大的道理来贯通我的所学罢了。”

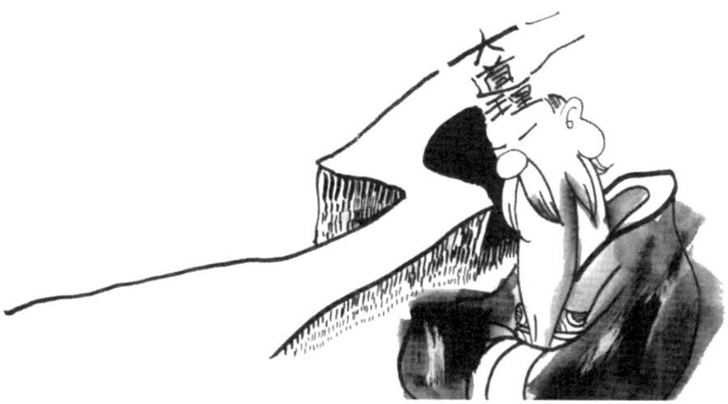


Confucius said to Zi Gong: “Do you think I have learned lots and am remembering everything?”
Zi Gong answered: “Yes, is that correct?”
Confucius said: “No, I am but uniting all my learnings with one connecting principle.”

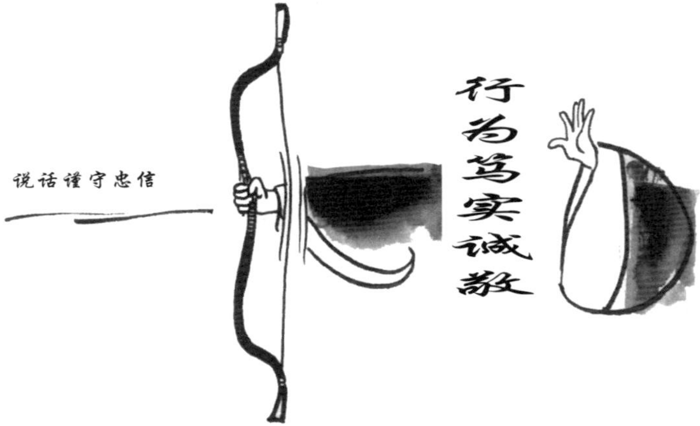


子张问行。

子曰:“言忠信,行笃敬,虽蛮貊之邦,行矣。言不忠信,行不笃敬,虽州里,行乎哉?立,则见其参于前也;在舆,则见其倚于衡也。夫然后行。”

子张书诸绅。

子张问孔子如何可以行得通。

孔子说:“如果你说话能够谨守忠信,行为笃实诚敬,不管你到哪里,就是蛮夷之地,也会行得通的。如果你说话不能谨守忠信,行为不是笃实诚信,就是你仍住在本乡本里,也能行得通吗?永远记住这种道理,不论你在站立的时候,或在乘车子的时候。如能做到,你就会到处行得通了。”

子张把这些话写在他的大带子上,以免忘记。

Zi Zhang asked how a man could conduct himself to get along well with others.

Confucius said: “Be sincere and conscientious when you speak to some one. Be earnest and serious when you do something. If you can do these, you will get along well with others even if you live in the most barbaric places. If you do not do these, even if you live in your own area, will you get along well? Keep these principles in mind all the time, whether you are standing or whether you are driving a carriage. These principles are right there inside yourself. With these, you will get along well with all people.”

Zi Zhang wrote Confucius' words of advice on his belt so he would be sure not to forget them.

子曰:“直哉史鱼!邦有道如矢,邦无道如矢。君子哉蘧伯玉!邦有道则仕,邦无道,则可卷而怀之。”

孔子说:“史官鱼这个人真是正直啊!政治清明时,他做事就像箭一样地直;政治黑暗时,他正言进谏也像箭一样地直。蘧伯玉这个人真是个君子啊!政治清明时,他为政府服务,政治黑暗时,他就归隐了。”

Confucius said: “What a straightforward historian Yu was! When there was justice and order in the government, his actions were as straight as arrows; when there was no justice and order in the government, his advices to the prince were as straight as arrows, too. What a superior man Qu Boyu was! When there was justice and order in the government, he worked for the government; when there was no justice and order in the government, he simply retired.”

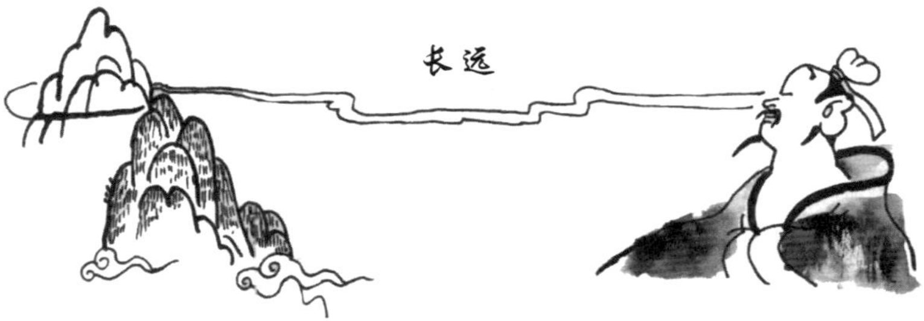


子曰:"人无远虑,必有近忧。"

孔子说:"如果一个人没有长远的思虑,他很快就会有事情忧愁的。"

Confucius said: " If a man does not have a long-term plan for himself, he will soon have something to worry about."

子曰:"躬自厚而薄责于人,则远怨矣。"

孔子说:"如果一个人经常检讨自己并严厉地去责备自己的过错,而对别人的过错只去轻微地指责,这样的人就不会被人怨恨了。"

Confucius said: "If a man questions himself frequently, looks at himself critically, and demands little from others, he will never be hated."

子曰:“不曰如之何如之何者,吾未如之何也已矣。”

孔子说:“遇到困难而不说怎么办怎么办的人,我对他也是没有办法的。”

Confucius said: “If a man confronts a problem and does not ask himself, ‘What can I do? What can I do?’ I don't know what I could do with the man.”

子曰:“群居终日,言不及义,好行小惠,难矣哉。”

孔子说:“整天聚集在一起,可就是不谈义理,而喜欢去做一些小聪明的事情。这种人是很难成就大事的。”

Confucius said: “When a group of people gather together all day and say nothing about righteousness, but show pettiness, It would be hard for them to make great achievements.”

子曰:“吾之于人也,谁毁谁誉?如有所誉者,其有所试矣。”

孔子说:“我对于一般人,谁应该褒贬?谁应该赞誉?我是很少去赞誉一个人的。如果我真的赞誉了一个人,那我对他的行为必定已经观察很久了。”

Confucius said: “ For the people, whom should I condemn? Whom should I praise? I do not praise people very often. If I do praise a person, I must have observed his conduct for a long time.”

子曰:“巧言乱德,小不忍则乱大谋。”

孔子说:“花言巧语会扰乱仁德。如果对于小忿不能忍耐,那会毁坏大事的。”

Confucius said: “Nice but diplomatic words may confuse people looking for virtue. If a man can not refrain from a small matter, he can ruin the big plan ahead.”

子曰:“众恶之,必察焉。众好之,必察焉。”

孔子说:“如果大家都厌恶这个人,我们必须研究为什么。如果大家都喜欢这个人,我们也应该研究为什么。”

Confucius said: “If the multitude disliked a certain person, we must examine the reasons why he was disliked. If the multitude liked a certain person, we must also examine the reasons why he was liked.”

子曰:“人能弘道,非道弘人。”

孔子说:“人可以弘扬正道,而不是让正道去弘扬人。”

Confucius said: “It is the people who raise the principle, not the principle that raises the people.”

子曰:“君子谋道不谋食。耕也,馁在其中矣。学也,禄在其中矣。君子忧道不忧贫。”

孔子说:“君子只担心大道之是否弘扬,而不担心有没有饭吃。譬如耕田的人应该不会没有饭吃的,不过如果遇到荒年,也会有饥饿的。一个人如能学成后在政府工作,就会有薪俸的。所以君子只担心是否能弘道,而不担心是否会贫穷。”

Confucius said: “A superior man only worries if the rightfulness practices, not about food. Farming will not lead to starvation, but sometimes it does because of drought . When a man receives a good education, he may work for the government and receive a salary. So a superior man only worries if the rightfulness practices, not poverty.”

子曰:“有教无类。”

孔子说:“教育应该没有贫富贵贱的类别。”

Confucius said: “Education should be done without the difference between the rich and the poor, or the noble and the mean.

子曰:"道不同,不相为谋。"

孔子说:"信仰不同,就无法相互商讨切磋。"

Confucius said: " Difference of beliefs makes people unable to study and discuss together."

子曰:"辞,达而已矣。"

孔子说:"说话是用来表达想要讲的事情,只要能说明白就可以了。"

Confucius said: "Language means to convey what we want to say. If we say clearly, that would be good."

孔子曰:"益者三友,损者三友。友直,友谅,友多闻,益矣。友便辟,友善柔,友便佞,损矣。"

孔子说:"与三种朋友往来会有益处,与三种朋友往来会有损害。交接正直的朋友,交接信实的朋友,交接知识广博的朋友,都会有益处的。交接喜欢巧辩的朋友,交接喜欢说奉承话的朋友,交接不诚实的朋友,都会有损害的。"

Confucius said: "Three kinds of people can be beneficial, while three other kinds of people can be injurious. If you befriend the people who are honest, faithful or knowledgeable, you will receive benefits from them. If you befriend the people who like to argue, or the people who like to say flattering words, or the people who is not honest, they are injurious."

孔子曰:“益者三乐,损者三乐。乐节礼乐,乐道人之善,乐多贤友,益矣。乐骄乐,乐佚游,乐宴乐,损矣。”

孔子说:“三种爱好对人有益处,三种爱好对人有害处。爱好用礼法及音乐来节制自己,爱好称扬别人的好处,爱好和贤德的人做朋友,这三种爱好都是有益处的。爱好骄奢逸乐,爱好游荡无度,爱好狂宴不节制,这三种爱好都是有害处的。”

Confucius said:“ Three kinds of pleasures are beneficial, and three other kinds of pleasures are injurious. The pleasures of using ceremonies and music to restrict oneself, of speaking of the goodness of others, and of making friendship with the people of virtue are all beneficial pleasures. The pleasures of dissipation, of extravagance, and of conviviality are all injurious.”

孔子曰:“侍于君子有三愆:言未及之而言,谓之躁;言及之而不言,谓之隐;未见颜色而言,谓之瞽。”

孔子说:“侍奉国君有三种容易犯的错误:他还没有问到而你就说了,这叫做急躁。他问你而你不说出来,这叫做隐瞒。没有观察他的脸色就随便乱说,这叫做盲瞎。”

Confucius said: “A man often makes three kinds of errors when he is with his prince: He speaks when his prince does not ask him to speak. This is called rashness. He does not speak when his prince asks him to speak. This is called concealment. He speaks without looking at his prince’s countenance. This is called blindness.”

孔子曰:“君子有三畏:畏天命,畏大人,畏圣人之言。小人不知天命而不畏也,狎大人,侮圣人之言。”

孔子说:“君子害怕这三种事:害怕违背天理,害怕违背居于高位的人,害怕违背圣人的教训。小人不知道也不害怕天理,不尊敬位居高位的人,藐视圣人的教训。”

Confucius said: “A superior man should hold three things in awe: ordinances of Heaven, persons in authority, and words of sages.An inferior man does not know the ordinances of Heaven and is not in awe of it, he is disrespectful of persons in authority, and he disdains the words of sages.”

孔子曰:“生而知之者,上也。学而知之者,次也。困而学之,又其次也。困而不学,民斯为下矣。”

孔子说:“天生就明白道理的人是上等的人,必须学习后才可以明白道理的人是次一等人,要努力去学习才可以明白道理的人是三等人。必须努力学习才可以明白道理,可是他不去学习当然就不明白道理,这种人应该是最下等的人了。”

Confucius said: “ Those who are born with knowledge are the highest class of people. Those who receive knowledge by studying are the second highest class of people. Those who are born dull, but study hard to attain knowledge, are the third highest class. Those, who are born dull, but do not study, and thus do not have knowledge, are the lowest class of people.”

子曰:“性,相近也;习,相远也。”

孔子说:“每个人的天性本来都是差不多的,因为后天的环境不同,于是便逐渐地不同了。”

Confucius said: “ By nature, all men are nearly alike when their lives begin. When they are growing, they become different from each other because of what they practice.”

子曰:“小子,何莫学夫《诗》?《诗》可以兴,可以观,可以群,可以怨。迩之事父,远之事君。多识于鸟兽草木之名。”

孔子说:“弟子们,你们为什么不去研读《诗经》?读《诗经》可以启发一个人的心志,可以增进一个人的观察力,可以教导人们如何相处,如何发泄怨恨,就近还可以教导人们如何事奉父母,就远也教导臣子如何事奉君主。此外,更可以知道小鸟野兽和各种草木的名称。”

Confucius said: “ Students, why don’t you study the *Book of Poetry*? Studying poetry will stimulate a person’s mind, improve a Person’s observation, teach a person how to be sociable, and regulate feelings of resentment. Studying poetry will teach you how to treat your parents at home, as well as how to serve your prince in the court. Meanwhile, it will also give you the chance to learn the names of birds, beasts, and plants.”

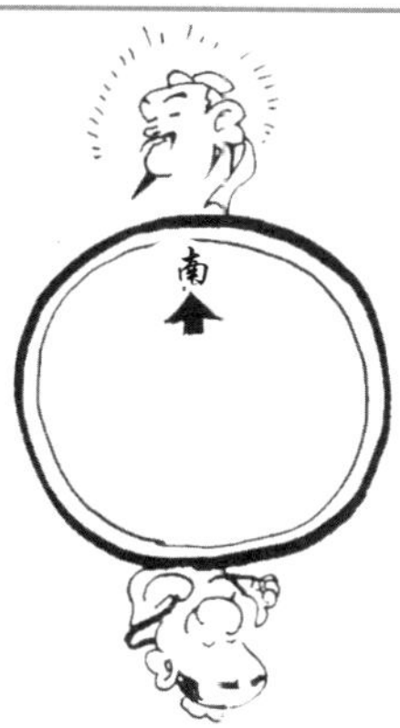


子曰:“唯上知与下愚不移。”

孔子说:“只有最聪明的人和最愚笨的人是不容易改变的。”

Confucius said: “The only ones who do not easily change are those of the highest wisdom and the lowest dullness.”

子谓伯鱼曰:“女为《周南》《召南》矣乎?人而不为《周南》《召南》,其犹正墙面而立也与。”

孔子问伯鱼(孔子的儿子):“你可曾读过《诗经》里的《周南》和《召南》两篇诗?一个人如果不去读《周南》和《召南》这两篇诗,就好像正面向着墙壁站立看不到什么东西。”

Confucius asked Bo Yu (Confucius' son) whether he had learned the poetry of *Zhou Nan* and *Zhao Nan*, "If a man never studied *Zhou Nan* and *Zhao Nan*, he would be like one who stands with his face to the wall, seeing nothing."

子曰:“礼云礼云,玉帛云乎哉。乐云乐云,钟鼓云乎哉。”

孔子说:“现在的所谓礼呀礼呀的,不过是送点玉帛之类的礼品而已。现在的所谓乐呀乐呀的,不过是敲敲钟打打鼓而已。”

Confucius said: " Nowadays, when people speak about rules of propriety, they would think that propriety merely means presenting of gems and silk. When people speak about music, they would think that music merely means beating the bells and drums."

子曰:“色厉而内荏,譬诸小人,其犹穿窬之盗也与。”

孔子说:“外表很威严,可是内心却很懦弱,这种人就好像小人及那些爬墙过壁的盗贼之流。”

Confucius said: “A man, who puts on a stern appearance but is weak and cowardly at heart, is but like an inferior person, a thief who breaks through a wall.”

子曰:“乡原,德之贼也。”

孔子说:“外貌忠诚,行为奸诈,这种人实在是仁德的败坏者。”

Confucius said: “ A man who looks faithful, but acts craftily is actually a destroyer of virtue.”

子曰:“道听而途说,德之弃也。”

孔子说:“在路上听到的话,不经考虑便将之传播。这种事是仁德之人所不为的。”

Confucius said: “ Picking up sayings in the public streets and preaching them without consideration is something a virtuous man does not do.”

子曰:“古者,民有三疾,今也或是之亡也。古之狂也肆,今之狂也荡。古之矜也廉,今之矜也忿戾。古之愚也直,今之愚也诈而已矣。”

孔子说:“古时候人民有三种毛病,现在可能没有了。古时候的志气高的人是不拘小节而已,现在的志气高的人是放荡太过。古时候高傲的人仍是廉洁的,现在高傲的人是脾气暴躁。古时候所谓愚笨的人仍很正直,现在所谓愚笨的人是只会欺诈。”

Confucius said: “In the early times, people had three kinds of imperfections which perhaps can not be found today. In the early times, the ambitious people did not pay much attention only when they handled the small points of virtue; today, those people are totally wild. In the early times, the proud people were still modest; today, those people all have bad temper. In the early times, the stupid people were still straight; today, those people are but cunning.”

子曰:“年四十而见恶焉,其终也已。”

孔子说:“到了四十岁了还被人厌恶,那这个人的一生便是如此了。”

Confucius said: “If a man at the age of forty still becomes a person of dislike, this man will not be able to change for the rest of his life.”

子曰:“不知命,无以为君子也。不知礼,无以立也。不知言,无以知人也。”

孔子说:“不知道天命,这个人便不配叫做君子。不知道礼法,便无法立身处世。不能够分辨好话坏话,便无法去了解人。”

Confucius said: “Without knowing the ordinances of Heaven, a man can not be called a superior man. Without knowing the rules of propriety, a man’s character can not be established. Without abilities to distinguish good words from bad ones, a man can not understand the other people.”

# 第四章
# CHAPTER FOUR

## 孔子，一位伟大的平民
## CONFUCIUS, A GREAT ORDINARY MAN

子曰“有朋自远方来,不亦乐乎?”

孔子说:“有朋友从很远的地方来看望,不是一件很快乐的事情吗?”

Confucius said: “Isn’t it delightful to have a friend coming to visit from a faraway place? ”

子曰:“吾十有五而志亍学, 三十而立, 四十而不惑, 五十而知天命, 六十而耳顺, 七十而从心所欲不逾矩。”

孔子说:“我十五岁时, 就立志去求取学问;到了三十岁时, 就把立身处世的方向看清了;到了四十岁时, 就不会被时尚邪说所迷惑;到了五十岁时, 我就明了了天命的奥义;到了六一岁时,耳朵一听到什么, 便会立刻明了那是对的还是错的;到了七十岁时,就能想到什么就做什么,而不会超越礼法。”

Confucius said: “ At fifteen, I made up my mind to study hard. At thirty, I made decision about what I was going to do in life. At forty, I would not be misled by the evil sayings. At fifty, I understood the natural law. At sixty, I could immediately understand what I heard was right or wrong. At seventy, I could do whatever my mind desired without going beyond what was right.”

仪封人请见，曰："君子之至于斯也，吾未尝不得见也。"
从者见之。
出曰："二三子，何患于丧乎？天下之无道也久矣，天将以夫子为木铎。"

当孔子一行人经过仪邑时，仪邑小吏请见孔子，对孔子的弟子们说："凡是君子来到这个地方，我没有不请求见面的。"
孔子的弟子把他带去见过了孔子。
出来后，他对孔子的弟子们说："你们为何要担心老师没有官职呢？天下混乱无道已经很久了，老天将会安排你们的老师出来做个醒世警钟的。"

A warden at a place called Yi asked to see Confucius while Confucius and his disciples were traveling through the area. The warden said: "Whenever a superior man comes here, I would always have an opportunity to see him."
So the disciples took him to see their master, Confucius.
After that, the warden said to the disciples: "Gentlemen, why are you worried about your master's not getting an office? The world has been long without order and justice. The Heaven is going to arrange for your master to be a BELL to awaken the world."

子谓韶尽美矣，又尽善矣。谓武尽美矣，未尽善也。

孔子认为韶乐是尽美又尽善的音乐。武乐虽然尽美，惟尚未尽善。

Confucius said of a famous piece of music, Shao, which had all the excellence of harmony, as well as the excellence of moral grandeur. As for Wu, another piece of famous music, it had all the excellence of harmony, but did not have the excellence of moral grandeur.

子谓公冶长可妻也，虽在缧绁之中，非其罪也。以其子妻之。

孔子认为公冶长将是一个好丈夫，虽然他曾经坐过牢，可是，他是无辜的，所以将他的女儿嫁给了他。

Confucius said of Gong Yezhang, he would be a good husband. Although he had been put in the jail, he was innocent. So Confucius married his daughter to Gong Yezhang.

子谓南容,邦有道不废;邦无道,免于刑戮;以其兄之子妻之。

孔子认为南容这个人,当政治清明时,他在政府内任职;当政治不清明时,他也可以免除祸难。所以孔子把他哥哥的女儿嫁给了他。

Confucius said of Nan Rong, he had a position in the government when the nation was well governed. When the nation was ill governed, he knew how to get rid of the troubles. So Confucius married his elder brother's daughter to Nan Rong.

子曰:"道不行,乘桴浮于海,从我者其由也与。"子路闻之喜。子曰:"由也,好勇过我。无所取材。"

孔子说:"如果我的政治理念行不通了,我将乘着木筏漂流到海上去,那时跟着我的人大概是仲由(子路)吧。"
子路听了很高兴。
孔子又说:"仲由这个人比我勇敢,可是我不知道如何弄到造木筏的材料。"

Confucius said: "Since my doctrines are not making their way on the land, I am thinking of getting upon a raft and floating about on the sea. If I do, the disciple who may accompany me will be Zi Lu."
Zi Lu was honored when he heard this. Confucius then said: "Zi Lu is braver than I. But how can we get the material to make such a raft?"

子谓子贡曰:“女与回也孰愈?”
对曰:“赐也,何敢望回。回也,闻一以知十。赐也,闻一以知二。”
子曰:“弗如也。吾与女弗如也。”

孔子问子贡:“你和颜回相比,哪个比较优秀?”
子贡说:“我哪敢和颜回相比。颜回可以闻一知十,我只能闻一知二而已。”
孔子说:“你不如他。我和你都不如他。”

Confucius asked Zi Gong, “Comparing yourself with Hui, who do you think is more superior?” Zi Gong answered: “How can I dare to compare myself with Hui? Hearing one point, Hui knows ten more, while I only know two more.”
Confucius agreed and said: “You are right. You can not compare with him. You and I both can not compare with him.”

子贡曰:“夫子之文章,可得而闻也。夫子之言性与天道,不可得而闻也。”

子贡说:“老师平日的言谈举止是有目共睹的。但是老师对人性与天道的讲授,还没有轻易听到过。”

Zi Gong said: “Our master’s principles of personal character and their descriptions have been heard. But our master’s explanations of human nature and the way of Heaven have not been easily heard yet.”

子路有闻未之能行，唯恐有闻。

当子路听到了一件有德行的事情而仍未能将之实行时，他就害怕再听到新的有德行的事情。

When Zi Lu heard about a virtuous thing and he had not yet practiced it, he would be afraid of hearing another new one.

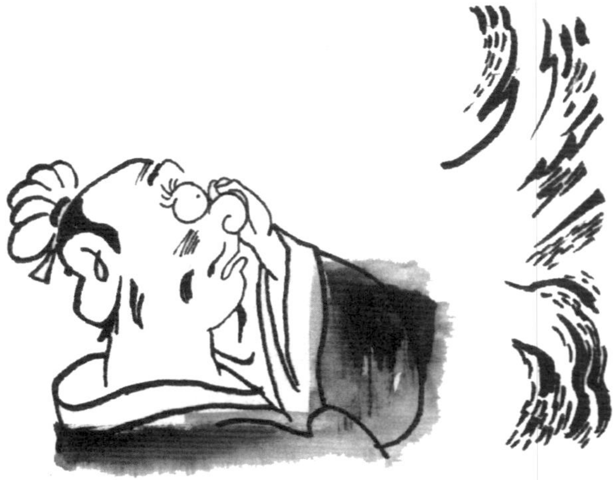

子在陈曰："归与！归与！吾党之小子狂简，斐然成章，不知所以裁之。"

当孔子在陈国时，他说："回去吧！回去吧！我的这班弟子们志气都很高大，而且文理也很有成就，可就是不能裁度事理。"

When Confucius was traveling in the State of Chen, he said: "I must consider going home! I must consider going home! My young disciples at home are ambitious and hasty. They have made some accomplishments, but they don't Know how to judge."

子曰:“十室之邑,必有忠信如丘者焉,不如丘之好学也。”

孔子说:“每十个人家中,就必定会有人和我一样忠信,不过可能不如我一样好学罢了。”

Confucius said: “In every place of ten families, there must be people as honest and faithful as I am, but they may not be as fond of learning as I am.”

伯牛有疾,子问之。自牖执其手,曰:“亡之,命矣夫!斯人也,而有斯疾也!斯人也,而有斯疾也!”

伯牛生了重病,孔子去看他。孔子从窗户中握住他的手,对他的家人说:“老天真是作弄人啊!怎么使这个人得了这么一个病!怎么使这个人得了这么一个病!”

Confucius' disciple, Bo Niu, had a serious disease. Confucius went to see his disciple. Holding the patient's hand through an outside window, Confucius said to his families: “What a decision the Heaven made for him! How could he have such a disease! How could he have such a disease!”

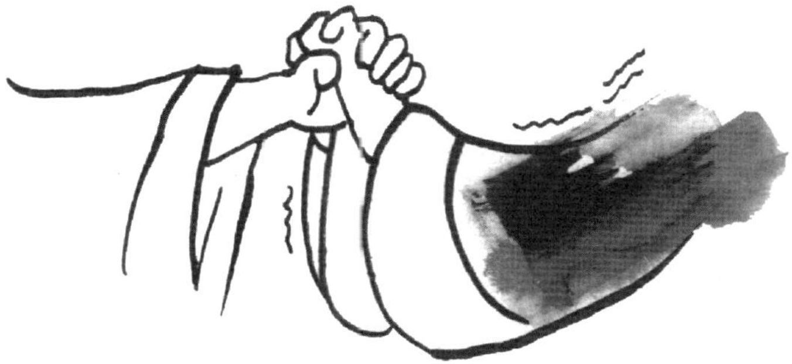

子见南子，子路不说。
夫子矢之曰："予所否者，天厌之，天厌之！"

当孔子去见美丽可是声名狼藉的国君宠姬南子时，子路不高兴。
孔子发誓说："如果我做得不对，请老天爷处罚我，请老天爷处罚我！"

On one occasion, Confucius paid a visit to Nan Zi, his prince's beautiful but notorious concubine. The visit made Confucius' disciple, Zi Lu, unhappy. Confucius explained: "If I have done it improperly, may Heaven punish me. May Heaven punish me!"

子曰："述而不作，信而好古，窃比于我老彭。"

孔子说："我只是传述旧闻，而不创新，我相信也喜欢古道，私心去效法前贤老彭。"

Confucius said: "I like to retell the old truth and am not a new theory maker. I believe in and am fond of the ancients. I hope I may compare myself with the old Worthy Peng."

子之燕居，申申如也，夭夭如也。

孔子在家闲居时，容态舒适，神情愉快。

Whenever Confucius had nothing to do at home, he would look easy and cheerful.

子食于有丧者之侧，未尝饱也。

当孔子在家有丧事的人旁边吃饭时，从未吃饱过。

Whenever Confucius was eating next to a person in mourning, he would not eat to his fullest.

子于是日哭，则不歌。

当孔子哭了的那天，他就不唱歌了。

If Confucius had wept, he would not sing on that day.

子之所慎：齐，战，疾。

当这三件事发生时，孔子就会非常小心谨慎：斋戒、战争和疾病。

Confucius wanted to exercise his greatest caution in these three moments: attending a worship, during a war, and being sick.

子在齐闻韶，三月不知肉味。曰："不图为乐之至于斯也。"

孔子在齐国听到了韶乐。他是如此地全神贯注，三个月来，甚至于连在吃饭时，都尝不出肉的美味了。他说："真想不到这音乐有如此之好听。"

When Confucius was in the State of Qi, he heard the ancient music of Shao. For three months, he was so bewitched by the music that he could not even distract his mind to taste the good flavor of meat when eating. He said: "I could never have imagined the music of Shao to be so wonderful!"

叶公问孔子于子路，子路不对。
子曰："女奚不曰：'其为人也，发愤忘食，乐以忘忧，不知老之将至云尔。'"

叶公问子路，孔子究竟是个什么样的人。子路没有回答。以后子路又把这事告诉孔子。孔子说："你为何不告诉他，'他这个人在发奋研究学问的时候，往往会连吃饭也忘记了。等到有了进步了，他又会高兴得忘记一切忧愁，而不知道自己已经进入老年的境界了。'"

The reigning prince of a small principality, Ye, asked Confucius' disciple, Zi Lu, what kind of person his master was. Zi Lu did not know How to reply, and later ontold his masterabout the question. Confucius said: "Why didn't you tell him, 'He is such a man who, in his eager pursuit of knowledge, often forgets to eat, and when he makes progress, he will be so joyful and forget all his sorrows without realizing that he is getting older already.'"

子钓而不网，弋不射宿。

孔子钓鱼时不用鱼网，只用鱼钩子。他打猎时，不去射那正在窝里睡觉的鸟。

Whenever Confucius went fishing, he used a rod and angle, never a net. Whenever Confucius went hunting, he would not shoot at a bird which was perching on a nest.

子与人歌而善，必使反之，而后和之。

孔子与人唱歌时，如那个人唱得好，他就会请那个人重唱一次，而他就和着一起唱。

Whenever Confucius was in company with a person who was singing very well, Confucius would ask the singer to repeat the song, and he himself would accompany the singer with his own voice.

子曰:"文,莫吾犹人也。躬行君子,则吾未之有得。"

孔子说:"关于文化方面的知识,我也许和别人差不多。至于实行君子之道,我还没有做到。"

Confucius said: "Concerning the knowledge of letters and arts, perhaps I am equal to others. But, carrying out the superior man's belief in conduct, I have not yet attained it."

子曰:"若圣与仁,则吾岂敢?抑为之不厌,诲人不倦,则可谓云尔已矣。"
公西华曰:"正唯弟子不能学也。"

孔子说:"谈到圣人和仁者,我怎么够资格?我不过在这个方面去努力弘扬而不觉得厌倦,教导别人朝这个方向努力也不嫌疲倦而已。"
公西华说:"这正是我们弟子不能学到的地方。"

Confucius said: " Looking toward being a sage and a man of perfect virtue, how dare I rank myself with them? I am but keeping to move toward that direction without feeling bothered, and I am also teaching people to move to that direction without weariness."
Gong Xihua said: "Those are the things that we, disciples, can not imitate in you."

子温而厉，威而不猛，恭而安。

孔子平日看来温和中带有严肃，有尊严但不凶猛，既恭敬又安详。

Confucius looked mild, but serious; dignified, yet not fierce; respectful and peaceful.

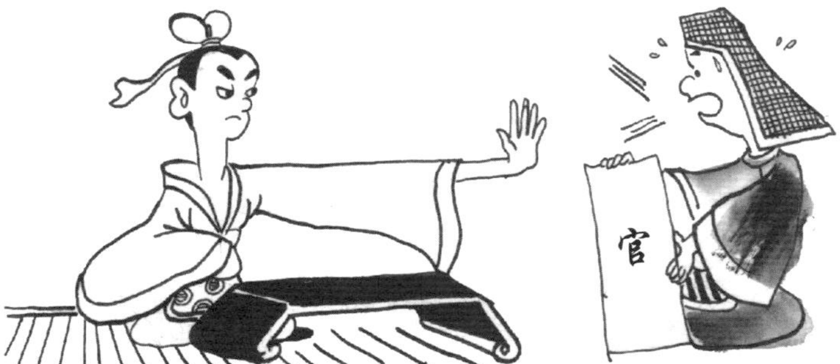


子曰："三年学不至于穀，不易得也。"

孔子说："努力去研究学问三年后仍然不想去做官的，这样的人现在已经不易多得了。"

Confucius said: "It is hard to find a man who has studied for three years and does not intend to find a position in the government."

达巷党人曰:“大哉孔子,博学而无所成名。”子闻之,谓门弟子曰:“吾何执,执御乎?执射乎?吾执御矣。”

达巷乡有人说:“孔子是伟大的,他的学问很广博,惟不专精,在任何一行学问上都不是一位专家。”孔子听了后对他的弟子们说:“我专心于什么呢?去驾车?还是去射箭?我想我去驾车好了。”

A man from Da Xiang Village said: “Confucius is great. His knowledge is so extensive, yet he has not distinguished himself in any one particular field.”
When Confucius heard of this, he said to his disciples, “What should I concentrate on? Should I concentrate on driving or archery? I think I should concentrate on driving.”

子畏于匡,曰:“文王既没,文不在兹乎。天之将丧斯文也,后死者不得与于斯文也。天之未丧斯文也,匡人其如予何?”

孔子和他的弟子们在经过匡地的时候,因为误会而处于极大的危机中。孔子说:“文王既已过世,发扬和推广文化的责任不就落到了我的头上了么。上天如果要丧失这文化,就不会要我这个后生参与他的文化。如果上天不要丧失这文化,那么匡人又能把我怎么样呢?”

When Confucius and his group traveled through a place called Kuang, a misunderstanding put him in great danger. Confucius said to his disciples: “Since the death of Emperor Wen, the responsibility of the extension of civilization has fallen upon me. If Heaven wants to destroy this civilization, the younger generation like me will not have a chance to receive it. If Heaven does not want to destroy this civilization, what can the people of Kuang do to me?”

大宰问于子贡曰:“夫子圣者与?何其多能也?”
子贡曰:“固天纵之将圣,又多能也。”
子闻之曰:“大宰知我乎!吾少也贱,故多能鄙事。君子多乎哉?不多也。”

有个官员问子贡:“你的老师是个圣人吧?他怎么这样多能呢?”
子贡说:“老天要他成为圣人,所以他又多能。”
孔子听了后说:“这官员真是知道我的呀!我年少时微贱,所以我能做很多微贱的事。一个君子是否要做很多微贱的事?不,他是不需要的。”

An official asked Zi Gong: “Is your master a sage? How can he do so many things?”
Zi Gong answered: “Heaven wants our master to be a sage. Therefore, he can do many things.”
When Confucius heard of the conversation, he said: “How could the official know me so well! When I was young, my status was low so I had to do many common matters. Must a superior man do many common matters? No, he does not.”

子贡曰:“有美玉于斯,韫匵而藏诸,求善贾而沽诸?”
子曰:“沽之哉,沽之哉,我待贾者也。”

子贡说:“假定这儿有块美玉,我们是把它藏在柜子里呢,还是等有好价钱就将之卖出呢?”
孔子说:“当然卖了,当然卖了。我是等有人出个好价钱就卖的。”

Zi Gong asked his master: “Suppose there were a piece of nice jade; should we hide it in a closet or try to sell it?”
Confucius answered: “Sell it. Sell it. I am ready to be sold for a good price.”

子欲居九夷。
或曰："陋，如之何？"
子曰："君子居之，何陋之有？"

孔子想搬到东方那九个文化不太高的民族一带去居住。
有人说："那儿太鄙陋了，如何能住？"
孔子说："如果一个君子搬去住了，怎么还会鄙陋呢？"

Confucius once wished to move and live with nine not very civilized tribes in the east. Someone told him: "They are rude people. How could you live with them?" Confucius said: "If a superior man lives with them, what rudeness would happen?"

子曰："吾自卫反鲁，然后乐正，雅颂各得其所。"

孔子说："我从卫国返回鲁国后，就把鲁国的音乐定正，使得雅乐和颂乐都有了应有的地位。"

Confucius said: "After I returned to my native state, Lu, from the state of Wei, I reformed the music in Lu in order that the royal songs and the praise songs both found their proper places."

子曰:"后生可畏,焉知来者之不如今也?四十五十而无闻焉,斯亦不足畏也矣。"

孔子说:"年轻的后辈是很有前途的,怎么知道他们将来会不如今日的我们呢?如果到了四十或五十岁时,仍然默默无闻,那也就不会再有什么前途了。"

Confucius said: " The younger generations have a great future. How do we know if their future is not as good as ours today? When a person reaches forty or fifty, and his name is still not well-known, he will indeed have no future."

孔子于乡党,恂恂如也,似不能言者。其在宗庙朝廷,便便言,唯谨尔。

孔子在乡亲中,说起话来结结巴巴的好像不太会说话似的;可是在宗庙里在朝廷上,他却说得很流畅,不过很谨慎。

Whenever Confucius was conversing with the neighbors or friends in his village, he spoke diffidently as if he were not a good speaker. Whenever he was in the prince's ancestral temple or the court, he spoke eloquently, but with caution.

食不语，寝不言。
虽疏食菜羹，必祭，必齐如也。

孔子在吃饭的时候是不多说话的，在要睡觉的时候也是不多说话的。即使吃的是简单的蔬菜一类的饭食，也要先拿出一点儿祭祀祖宗，而且在祭祀时是必恭必敬的。

While Confucius was eating, he would not talk much. Likewise, when he was about to sleep, he would not talk much.
Although his food might be only coarse rice and some simple vegetable dishes, he would always offer a little of it in sacrifice and do it respectfully.

席不正不坐。

孔子在座席没有放端正时是不坐下的。

Unless the mat used as a cushion was properly and squarely positioned, Confucius would not sit on the mat.

乡人饮酒，杖者出，斯出矣。乡人傩，朝服而立于阼阶。

孔子与乡间邻居们饮酒时，必须等扶着拐杖的年老人走了，他才走。当乡间举行驱鬼的队伍经过时，他将穿着上朝的衣服站立在家门前的左台阶上。

Whenever Confucius drank with his villagers, he left only after the seniors had left.In attending the local ceremonies to drive away the evil, when the procession of villagers passed through his house, Confucius would dress up in full uniform and stand on the left-hand side of the steps in front of his house to greet them.

问人于他邦，再拜而送之。

当孔子托人顺便问候他在其他国家的亲友时，他一定向这个人一拜又再拜，然后才送别。

Whenever Confucius sent complimentary inquiries to a friend in a foreign nation, he would bow twice while he said farewell to the messenger.

厩焚。子退朝,曰:“伤人乎?”不问马。

孔子从朝廷中回家后知道他家的马房被火烧了,他连忙问:“有人被烧伤吗?”他没有问马是否被烧伤了。

One day, when Confucius returned home from attending the court, he learned that his stable had just burned down. He asked immediately, “Anybody got hurt? ” He did not ask about the horses.

朋友死,无所归,曰:“于我殡。”

当孔子的一个朋友死亡了而没有亲人去收殓时,孔子就会说:“我来办理吧。”

Whenever a friend of Confucius died, and the dead friend had no families or relatives to be in charge of the funeral, Confucius would say: “ Let me take care of it.”

寝不尸。

孔子睡觉的时候，不会直挺挺地像个死尸一样地睡。

Whenever Confucius was in bed, he would not lie straight on his back to avoid looking like a corpse.

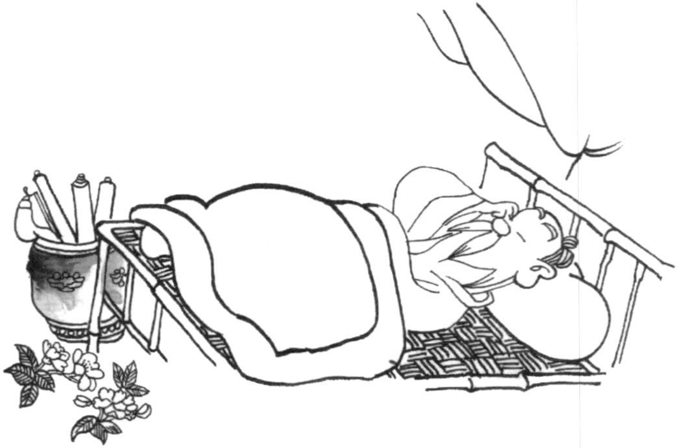

居不客。

孔子在家闲居时，衣着随便，不会像个客人似的。

At home, Confucius would not dress up like a guest.

见齐衰者，虽狎必变。见冕者与瞽者，虽亵必以貌。

当孔子见到身穿丧服的人，虽是熟人，他也会严肃起来的。当他见到政府官员身穿礼服或者瞎子时，虽然是常相见的人，他也会端庄起来的。

Whenever Confucius saw a person in mourning clothes, though the person might be an acquaintance, he would change countenance. Whenever Confucius saw a government official in full uniform or a blind person, even though he often saw the person, he would still behave himself with good manners.

凶服者式之。

当孔子乘车在路上遇见了治丧行列，他定会将头低下俯在他车前的横木上弯腰表示敬意。

Riding in his carriage, whenever Confucius met a funeral cortege, he would lean his head forward out of the carriage to bow.

有盛馔，必变色而作。

当孔子被邀请赴宴时，每道正菜上桌时，他都要站起来向主人致谢。

Whenever Confucius was invited to dinner, when a formal dish was brought to the table, he would rise up to thank the host.

迅雷，风烈，必变。

当孔子遇到响雷或暴风时，他的态度一定变得很严肃。

Whenever Confucius heard a sudden clap of thunder or a violent wind, he would change countenance and look serious.

升车，必正立，执绥。车中不内顾，不疾言，不亲指。

孔子坐上车子后便会端正站立，手握车绳。车子在行驶中，不回头向车内观望，不大声说话，也不用手向外东指西指。

After Confucius had mounted his carriage, he would stand straight and hold the cord. While the carriage was moving, he would not turn his head around, or talk hastily or point with fingers.

子曰："从我于陈、蔡者，皆不及门也。"

孔子说："当年跟随着我在陈、蔡两国受困的弟子们都已经不在身边了。"

Confucius said: "The disciples who followed me and shared hardships with me in Chen and Cai have not been with me now."

子畏于匡，颜渊后。
子曰：“吾以女为死矣。”
曰：“子在，回何敢死？”

当孔子在匡的地方遭难时，大家走散了，颜渊最后赶到了。
孔子对颜渊说：“我以为你已经遇害了。”
颜渊说：“有老师你在，我怎敢先死呢？”

When Confucius and his group were in danger in Kuang, his disciple, Yan Yuan, was separated from the group. Later on, Yan Yuan found his master and the other disciples.
Confucius said to Yan Yuan: “I was afraid you might have been killed.”
Yan Yuan answered: “While you are alive, how can I dare to die?”

德行：颜渊，闵子骞，冉伯牛，仲弓。
言语：宰我，子贡。政事：冉有，季路。文学：子游，子夏。

孔子的弟子中有德行的是：颜渊、闵子骞、冉伯牛和仲弓。有言语天才的是：宰我、子贡。有政治才干的是：冉有、季路。精通文艺的是：子游、子夏。

Among Confucius' disciples, Yan Yuan, Min Ziqian, Ran Boniu, and Zhong Gong were distinguished for their virtuous practice; Zai Wo and Zi Gong were distinguished for their abilities in making speeches; Ran You and Ji Lu were distinguished for their administrative abilities; Zi You and Zi Xia were distinguished for their literary arts.

子曰:“回也,非助我者也,于吾言无所不说。”

孔子说:“因为颜回从不发问使我加紧研究,所以他没有帮助我增进学问;不论何时他对我所说的都表示喜欢。”

Confucius said: “As Yan Hui never asked me questions to make me study hard, he did not help me improve myself. Whenever I talked with him, he always showed delight.”

子曰:“孝哉闵子骞,人不间于其父母昆弟之言。”

孔子说:“闵子骞真是一个孝顺父母的人,别人很难发现他的父母和他的兄弟之间所说的关于他的话有什么不同之处。”

Confucius said: “Min Ziqian is indeed a filial son. People can find no difference between what his parents and his brothers said of him.”

南容三复《白圭》,孔子以其兄之子妻之。

南容三番五次地诵读《白圭》这篇诗,孔子就把他哥哥的女儿嫁给了他。

Nan Rong was fond of reciting the poem *White Scepter*. Confucius married his elder brother's daughter to him.

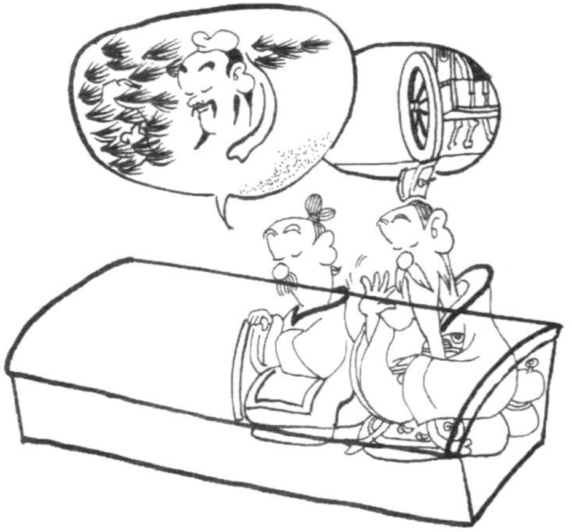

颜渊死,颜路请子之车以为之椁。子曰:"才,不才,亦各言其子也。鲤也死,有棺而无椁,吾不徒行以为之椁,以吾从大夫之后,不可徒行也。"

颜渊死了后,他的父亲颜路请求孔子把车子卖了,替他的儿子买一个外椁。孔子说:"不管儿子有才或无才,做父亲的都疼爱儿子。我的儿子鲤当初死了后也没有椁。我不能为了买椁而卖去我的车子去步行,因为我列名在大夫后面,出门时不可以没有车子代步。"

When Yan Yuan died, his father, Yan Lu, begged Confucius to sell carriage to buy an outer case for his son's coffin.
Confucius said: "Everybody loves his son whether the son has talents or not. When my son, Li, died, I did not buy him an outer case for his coffin. As I had the honor to be listed after the officials, I could not go out on foot without a carriage."

颜渊死，子曰："噫，天丧予！天丧予！"

颜渊死了，孔子痛哭着说："唉，这真是老天要亡我啊！真是老天要亡我啊！"

When Yan Yuan died. Confucius cried sadly: "Heaven destroys me! Heaven destroys me!"

颜渊死，子哭之恸。
从者曰："子恸矣！"
曰："有恸乎？非夫人之为恸而谁为？"

颜渊死了，孔子哭得非常伤心。
他的弟子们说："老师，你太伤心了！"
孔子说："我真的太伤心了吗？可我不为这个人哀痛，还去为谁哀痛呢？"

When Yan Yuan died, Confucius cried so mournfully that his other disciples said: "Master, your grief is excessive!" Confucius replied: "Is it excessive? If I am not mourning for this man, whom should I mourn for?"

子路、曾皙、冉有、公西华侍坐。
子曰:“以吾一日长乎尔,毋吾以也。
居则曰:‘不吾知也。’如或知尔,则何以哉?”
子路率尔而对曰:“千乘之国,摄乎大国之间,加之以师旅,因之以饥馑,由也为之,比及三年,可使有勇,且知方也。”
夫子哂之。“求,尔何如?”
对曰:“方六七十,如五六十,求也为之,比及三年,可使民足,如其礼乐,以俟君子。”
“赤,尔何如?”
对曰:“非曰能之,愿学焉。宗庙之事,如会同,端章甫,愿为小相焉。”
“点,尔何如?”
鼓瑟希铿尔,舍瑟而作,对曰:“异乎三子者之撰。”
子曰:“何伤乎,亦各言其志也。”
曰:“莫春者,春服既成,冠者五六人,童子六七人,浴乎沂,风乎舞雩,咏而归。”
夫子喟然叹曰:“吾与点也。”
三子者出,曾皙后。曾皙曰:“夫三子者何如?”
子曰:“亦各言其志也已矣。”
曰:“夫子何哂由也?”
曰:“为国以礼,其言不让,是故哂之。”
“唯求则非邦也与?”
“安见方六七十如五六十而非邦也者?”
“唯赤则非邦也与?”
“宗庙会同,非诸侯而何?
赤也为之小,孰能为之大?”

有一天，孔子和他的四个弟子子路、曾皙、冉有和公西华坐着闲谈。

孔子说："不要因为我比你们的年纪大就不敢说出你们的志向。你们平时不是时常说：'别人不知道我的能力。'如果有人知道了，你们会怎样呢？"

子路匆忙地说："如果有一个有千辆兵车的大国，而这个大国又夹在两个大国之间。同时，这个大国正面临着别的国家侵略，而自家的国内又闹着饥荒，如果由我来主理政务，三年之内，我可以使这个国家的人民勇敢地对抗侵略，也知道如何去照义理办事。"

孔子听了后微微一笑。接着孔子问冉有："你怎么说呢？"

冉有说："如果有个六七十里或者五六十里的地方由我来治理，三年以后，就可以使人民生活富足；至于说兴礼作乐这方面，我还是等那有才德的君子来做吧。"

孔子又问公西华："你怎么说呢？"

公西华说："我不敢说能够如何如何，可我愿意学习去做。譬如宗庙祭祀方面的事，两国国君相会时，或是有别的国君来访时，必须穿着礼服站在朝廷上，我可以做个赞礼的小相。"

孔子又问曾皙："你又怎么说？"

曾皙正在鼓瑟，听到孔子问他，把瑟音间歇了下来，随即发出铿的一声，放下瑟站了起来，说道："我的愿望和他们三个人不同。"

孔子说："这有什么关系呢，不过各人说说自己的志向罢了。"

曾皙说："在晚春的时候，我们穿着春天的衣服，与五六个成年人，六七个童子，在那沂水边洗洗手洗洗脚，在雨坛下乘乘风凉，然后唱着歌儿一同回家。"

孔子喟然叹道："我赞同曾皙的意见。"

等到子路、冉有和公西华三个人走出去后，曾皙留在后面，问孔子："他们三个人说得如何？"

孔子说："也不过各人说说自己的志向罢了。"

曾皙又问："那么老师为什么笑仲由呢？"

孔子说："治理国家要有礼法的，他说话太不谦逊，所以我笑他。"

曾皙又问："难道冉求所说的就不是国家了吗？"

孔子说："冉求是谦虚，怎见得六七十里或五六十里的地方就不是一个邦国呢？"

曾皙又问："难道公西华所说的就不是国家了吗？"

孔子说："公西华更谦虚了。宗庙会同这些事都是国家大事。公西华说他愿意做个小相，那么谁又可以做大相呢？"

Confucius' four disciples, Zi Lu, Zeng Xi, Ran You, and Gong Xihua were sitting in attendance on their master one day.
Confucius said: "Don't think because I am older than you, you dare not tell me your ambitions. You have often said, 'People do not know my ability.' If people knew your ability, what would you do?"
Zi Lu hastily said: "If a large nation, located between two large nations, were attacked by the Enemies; meanwhile, the nation were suffering from famine, let me conduct the state affairs for three years, I could make the people brave enough to defend their nation, and they would follow the rules in righteous ways."
Confucius smiled, then turned to Ran You, saying: "What would you say?"
Ran You said, "If it were a place of sixty or seventy square miles, or fifty or sixty square miles, let me handle the political affairs for three years. I could make the people live plentifully. As for the principles of propriety and music, I would wait for a superior man to come to do those things."
Confucius then said to Gong Xihua: "What would you like to say?"
Gong Xihua said: "I would not say I have much ability, but I would like to learn. At the services of the ancestral temple, and at the meetings of two princes, or receiving a prince from other nation, I think I could dress up and act as a small assistant at court."
Confucius then said to Zeng Xi: "What do you want to say?"
Zeng Xi was playing his lute, then slowed down and finally stopped playing and put aside the instrument, standing, saying: "My wish is different from the other three persons."
"It does not matter," Confucius said: "everybody states his own wishes."
Zeng Xi said: "In the late spring, I would like to wear spring clothes, go out with five or six adult friends and six or seven children, wash hands and feet in the River of Yi, and enjoy the breeze under the rain altar. When we return, we would be singing along the road."
Confucius answered with a sigh: "I agree with Zeng Xi."
Later, when the first three disciples went out while Zeng Xi stayed behind, Zeng Xi asked Confucius: "What do you think of the three people's ambitions?"
Confucius said: "They simply stated their ambitions."
Zeng Xi asked again: "Why did you smile at Zi Lu?"
Confucius said: "Governing a state demands the rules of propriety. Zi Lu was not humble, so I smiled at him."
Zeng Xi asked again, "Isn't what Ran Qiu said of a nation too?"
Confucius said, "Ran Qiu was humble. With a square mileage of sixty or seventy, fifty or sixty, isn't that a small nation?"
Zeng Xi asked again, "Didn't Gong Xihua also speak about a nation?"
Confucius said, "Gong Xihua was more humble. At the services of an ancestral temple and at the meetings of two princes, or receiving a prince from other nation, they are all state affairs. Gong Xihua said he could only be a small assistant. Then who would be a great assistant?"

颜渊死，门人欲厚葬之，子曰：“不可。”门人厚葬之。
子曰：“回也，视予犹父也，予不得视犹子也。非我也，夫二三子也。”

颜渊死了，孔子的其他弟子们要以隆重的葬礼去安葬，孔子说：“不必要。”结果，这些弟子们还是以厚礼把他安葬了。
孔子对他的弟子们说：“颜回(颜渊)待我像父亲一样，可我没有把他待若儿子。我没有以厚礼去安葬他，是你们以厚礼去安葬他的。”

When Yan Yuan died. Confucius’ disciples wanted to give him a grand funeral. Confucius said: “Not necessary.”
Nevertheless, the other disciples still gave him one.
Confucius said to his disciples: “Yan Hui (also Yan Yuan) treated me like his father, but I did not treat him like my son. I did not give him a grand funeral. It was you who gave him a grand funeral.”

子路无宿诺。

子路答应人家做的事多会立刻去做，不要等到第二天才去做。

When Zi Lu made a promise, he would try to carry it out right away without waiting for the next day.

子曰:"听讼,吾犹人也。必也使无讼乎。"

孔子说:"听断一件诉讼案子,我也能赶得上别人。可我最希望的是能够没有诉讼的事情发生。"

Confucius said: " Listening to the arguments of a dispute, I can decide the settlement as well as others. But my thought is that how wonderful it would be if there were no disputes at all."

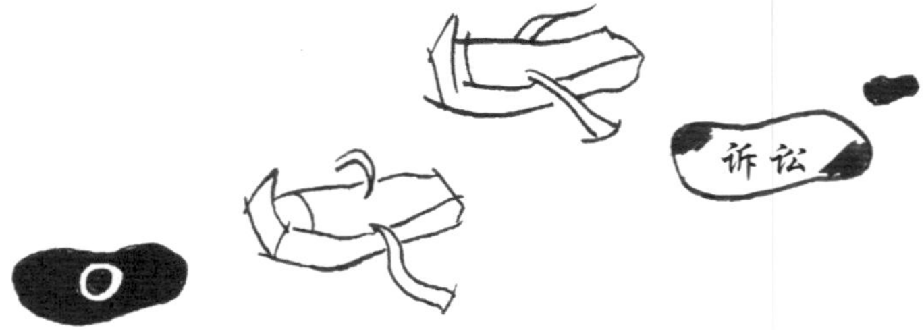

蘧伯玉使人于孔子。孔子与之坐而问焉,曰:"夫子何为?"
对曰:"夫子欲寡其过,而未能也。"使者出。子曰:"使乎!使乎!"

蘧伯玉派个使者来问候孔子。孔子与使者坐下后,问使者道:"你的主人最近做些什么?"
使者说:"我的主人只想如何去减少过失,可还没有达到呢。"
使者走后,孔子说:"好一个使者呀!好一个使者呀!"

Qu Boyu sent a messenger with friendly inquiries to Confucius. After having welcomed the messenger, Confucius asked, "What has your master been doing lately?"
The messenger answered, "My master is trying to correct the mistakes he has made, but he has not been successful yet."
After the messenger left, Confucius said, "What a nice messenger! What a nice messenger he is!"

微生亩谓孔子曰：“丘，何为是栖栖者与，无乃为佞乎？”
孔子曰：“非敢为佞也。疾固也。”

微生亩问孔子道：“孔丘啊，你为什么如此地到处忙碌呢，难道为了要炫耀你的口才吗？”
孔子说：“我不是为了要炫耀口才，实在是恨世人如此地固执啊。”

Wei Sengmu said to Confucius: “Qiu (Confucius’ first name), why are you traveling around so much? Does it mean that you want to show people you are a good speaker? ”
Confucius replied, “I don’t want to show people I am a good speaker. I just hate the persons of narrow-minded bigotry.”

子曰：“莫我知也夫。”
子贡曰：“何为其莫知子也？”
子曰：“不怨天，不尤人，下学而上达。知我者，其天乎！”

孔子说：“可能没有人知道我。”
子贡说：“怎么会没有人知道你呢？”
孔子说：“我从不埋怨老天，也不去乱怪别人。我从浅近处学习，向上面去领悟。因此，真正知道我的，大概只有老天吧！”

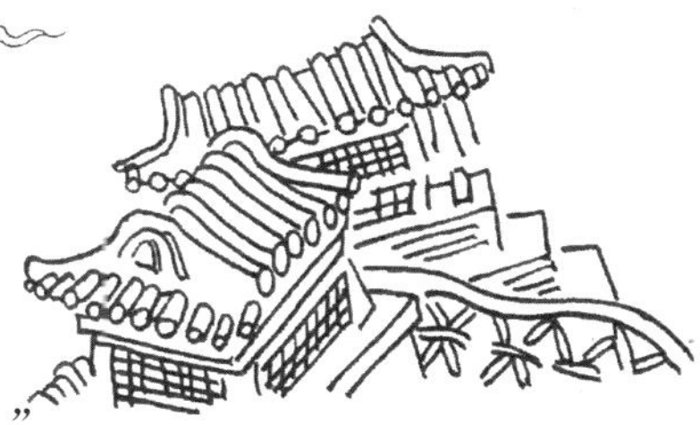

Confucius said, “Probably nobody really knows me.”
Zi Gong said, “How could it be that nobody really knows you? ”
Confucius said, “I don’t complain of the Heaven. I don’t complain of the people. My studies are on lowly things, but my thoughts penetrate the sublime. Perhaps, only the Heaven really knows me! ”

子路宿于石门。
晨门曰:“奚自?”
子路曰:“自孔氏。”
曰:“是知其不可而为之者与?”

子路在石门这个地方住宿。
守城门的一个小吏问子路:“从哪儿来的?”
子路说:“从孔氏那儿来。”
小吏说:“是明知不可以做到而仍在做的那个人吗?”

Zi Lu stayed one night in Shi Men.
The gatekeeper asked Zi Lu where he came from. Zi Lu answered, “From Confucius.”
The gatekeeper said, “Is he that man who knows what he is doing is impractical, but he still wants to do it? ”

子击磬于卫,有荷蒉而过孔氏之门者,曰:“有心哉击磬乎。”既而曰:“鄙哉硁硁乎。莫己知也,斯已而已矣。‘深则厉,浅则揭。’”
子曰:“果哉,末之难矣。”

孔子在卫国,有一天他敲磬自娱,恰巧有一个担着草笼的人走过孔子的门前。当他听到了孔子的磬声说:“这个击磬的人有个好心肠啊。”然后他又说:“你的见识却很有限啊。既然没有人知道你这个苦心,你就应该停止。《诗经》上不是说过吗,‘遇到深水的地方,就应该游水过去,遇到浅水的地方,就应当拉起裤管涉水过去。’”孔子听了后自语道:“说得好干脆。如果是这样,那也就没有困难了。”

Confucius was playing a musical instrument one day at his house in Wei. A man, carrying a straw basket, passed by the door of the house. The man said: “The musician's heart is full.” Then he said again: “It is a pity your knowledge is limited. When nobody takes any notice of you, you should stop. The *Book of Poetry* says, ‘When the water is high, you must swim over it. When the water is low, you can pull up your trousers and walk across it.’ ”
On hearing these words, Confucius said to himself: “It is easy to say it. If so, there would be no difficulties.”

原壤夷俟。
子曰:“幼而不孙弟,长而无述焉,老而不死是为贼。”以杖叩其胫。

原壤蹲踞着在等孔子。
孔子回来看到后,说:“年轻时做人不谦虚,到了年长也没有什么可以称颂的。这样的人到了老年时还没有死,真可以叫做贼啊。”
说完了,孔子用手杖去轻敲原壤的脚胫骨。

Yuan Rang squatted on his legs while he was waiting for Confucius.
When Confucius came, Confucius scolded: “In Youth, the person was not humble; in manhood, he did not do any things of worth.When he is in old age and still lives, the man may be called a rascal.”Then Confucius used his stick to hit Yuan Rang’s leg.

子曰:“由,知德者鲜矣。”

孔子对他的学生子由说:“由呀,明了什么是仁德的人可真少啊。”

Confucius said to his disciple, Zi You: “ You, not many persons really know what the virtue means.”

在陈绝粮,从者病,莫能兴。子路愠,见曰:“君子亦有穷乎?”
子曰:“君子固穷,小人穷斯滥矣。”

孔子在陈国时一度断绝了粮食供应,跟随着他的人都饥饿得像生了病似的而不能站立起来。子路很不高兴。他见孔子,问道:“君子也会困穷吗?”
孔子说:“君子困穷时仍能固守原则,小人困穷时就会什么事情都可以做得出来。”

Once when Confucius and his party reached Chen, their provisions were exhausted. His followers were so hungry that they could hardly stand up. Zi Lu was not happy. He came and asked Confucius: “Could a superior man also suffer this way?”
Confucius said: “When a superior man has some bad times, he can still stick to the principles. But when an inferior man suffers, he will become reckless and do whatever he wants.”

师冕见。
及阶，子曰："阶也。"
及席，子曰："席也。"
皆坐，子告之曰某在斯，某在斯。
师冕出，子张问曰："与师言之道与？"
子曰："然，固相师之道也。"

瞎眼音乐师名冕来见孔子。
当他走到台阶时，孔子就说："这里是台阶。"
当他走到座席时，孔子就说："这里是座席。"
等到大家都坐定了，孔子就说某人在这里，某人在那里。
乐师走了后，子张问孔子道："刚才和乐师说的都是应该的吗？"
孔子说："这本来就是帮助瞎眼乐师的道理么。"

The blind master musician, Mian, visited Confucius.
When he reached the steps, Confucius reminded him, "Here are the steps."
When he reached the seat, Confucius said, "Here is a seat."
After everybody was seated, Confucius introduced him to each person and told him where each person was seated.
After the musician left, Zi Zhang asked, "Is this the right way to behave toward a master musician?"
Confucius replied: "Yes, it is the right way to help a blind musician."

陈亢问于伯鱼曰:“子亦有异闻乎?”
对曰:“未也。尝独立,鲤趋而过庭,曰:‘学诗乎?’
对曰:‘未也。’‘不学诗,无以言。’鲤退而学诗。
他日又独立,鲤趋而过庭,曰:‘学礼乎?’对曰:‘未也。’
‘不学礼,无以立。’鲤退而学礼。闻斯二者。”
陈亢退而喜曰:“问一得三。闻诗闻礼,又闻君子之远其子也。”

陈亢问孔子的儿子伯鱼说:“你可曾受过你父亲特别的教导?”
伯鱼说:“没有啊。不过有一次,当父亲一个人站在那儿时,我适从他的身边穿过庭院,他问我:‘你学过诗吗?’我回答:‘还没有。’他说:‘一个人如不去学诗,言语就不能通达。’我以后就去学诗。又有一次,当他一个人站在那儿时,我适从他的身边穿过庭院,他问我:‘学过礼仪吗?’我回答:‘还没有。’他说:‘一个人如不学礼仪,将来就不会立身处世。’我以后就去学习礼仪。我就是受过父亲这两个教诲。”陈亢听了后很高兴,说:“我只问一个问题,却得到了三个答案。我知道了学诗和学礼的重要,又知道了君子是如何地教导他的儿子的。”

Chen Kang asked Bo Yu, Confucius’ son: “Have you heard some special lessons from your father? ”
Bo Yu said: “ No. But once when my father was standing by himself, I passed by him below the hall. He asked me whether I had learned the poetry. I answered: ‘Not yet.’ My father then said, ‘If you do not learn the poetry, you will not be agreeable in conversation with others.’ So I decided to learn poetry. The other day, when he was standing by himself and I was passing by him below the hall again, he asked me whether I had learned the rules of propriety. I answered, ‘Not yet.’ He said, ‘If you do not learn the rules of propriety, you will lack judgment and taste.’ So I decided to learn the rules of propriety. I have learned these two things from my father.”
After hearing Bo Yu’s statement, Chen Kang was very happy. He said: “I asked only one question, and I received three lessons. I learned the importance of learning poetry, the importance of learning rules of propriety, and how a superior man teaches his son.”

阳货欲见孔子，孔子不见。归孔子豚。
孔子时其亡也，而往拜之，遇诸涂。
谓孔子曰："来，予与尔言。曰：怀其宝而迷其邦，可谓仁乎："曰："不可。"
"好从事而亟失时，可谓知乎？"
曰："不可。"
"日月逝矣，岁不我与。"
孔子曰："诺，吾将仕矣。"

阳货想见孔子，可是孔子不想见他。阳货乃送给孔子一头猪。孔子等阳货不在家的时候去拜谢。想不到在路上遇到了阳货。
阳货对孔子说："过来，我有话要问你。如果一个人怀着才能，却不来挽救自己的国家，这个人还能算是个仁者吗？"
孔子说："这是不可以的。"
阳货又问："本来就喜欢替国家办事情，可是却屡次失去机会，这个人还能算是个智者吗？"
孔子说："不可以的。"
阳货说："时间过得很快，岁月是不饶人的。"
孔子说："是的，我将要出去从政了。"

Yang Huo wanted to see Confucius, but Confucius did not want to see him. Yang sent a pig to Confucius as a gift. Confucius went to Yang's house to say thanks while he assumed Yang would not be home by that time. The two men met on the way.
Yang said to Confucius, "Come over. I want to talk to you. If a man hides the treasures of his knowledge and let his nation go astray, can he still be called a man of virtue?"
Confucius answered: "No."
Yang asked: "If a man liked to do some things for his nation, but he often missed the opportunities to do them, can he still be called a man of wisdom?"
Confucius answered, "No."
Yang said, "The days and months are passing away. The years will not wait for us."
Confucius said, "That's right. I am going to work for the government."

公山弗扰以费畔, 召, 子欲往。子路不说, 曰: “末之也已, 何必公山氏之之也?”
子曰: “夫召我者, 而岂徒哉? 如有用我者, 吾其为东周乎?”

公山弗扰在费地反叛, 召孔子, 孔子想去, 子路很不高兴, 说: “你没有什么地方去就算了, 何必要到公山氏那儿去?”
孔子说: “难道他没有诚意邀请我么? 如果有人用我, 难道我就不能把这个地方治理得像东周一样好么?”

When Gongshan Furao was holding Fei, a city, in an attitude of rebellion, he invited Confucius to work for him. When Confucius wanted to accept his invitation, his disciple, Zi Lu, did not agree, saying: “If you have no place to go, that is all right. Why do you want to go to Gongshan's place?”
Confucius said, “Didn't he have a good reason to invite me? If somebody would employ me, could I not make the region as good as Eastern Zhou?”

佛肸召，子欲往。
子路曰："昔者，由也闻诸夫子曰：'亲于其身为不善者，君子不入也。'佛肸以中牟畔，子之往也，如之何？"
子曰："然，有是言也。不曰：'坚乎，磨而不磷，'不曰：'白乎，涅而不缁？'吾岂匏瓜也哉？焉能系而不食？"

佛肸请孔子去，孔子想去。
子路说："我以前听你说过，'如果这个人专做恶事，有道德的君子是不去的。'佛肸如今占据中牟地方反叛，你却想到那里去，那怎么可以呢？"
孔子说："是的，我是说过的。不过，你有没有也听说过，'那真正坚固的东西是怎么磨也磨不薄的'，'那真正白色的东西是怎么染也染不黑的？'我岂是一个匏瓜吗？只能挂着而不能吃吗？"

Fu Xi invited Confucius to see him and Confucius desired to go.
Zi Lu said: "I heard you once said, 'If a man is doing evil things, a superior man will not go to him.' Fu Xi is now holding Zhong Mo in rebellion. How could you go to see him?"
Confucius said, "Yes, I did say that. But, have you also heard the saying, 'If an object is really hard, it may not be ground thin,' and 'if a thing is really white, it may not be dyed black?' Am I a bitter gourd? How can I be hung up only without being eaten?"

阙党童子将命。或问之曰:“益者与?”
子曰:“吾见其居于位也,见其与先生并行也,非求益者也 欲速成者也。”

阙党地方的一个童子在替孔子做些传达话语的工作。有人问孔子:“这个小孩还有点进步吗?”孔子说:“我看到他喜欢坐在大人坐的位子上,我看到他喜欢与大人并排着走路。他不是来求进益的,他很想快点儿长大。”

A youth from a place called Que Dang was employed by Confucius to carry messages between him and his visitors. Someone asked Confucius: “Is the boy making some progress?”
Confucius said: “I noticed that he was fond of taking the seat of a grown-up man. I noticed that he tried to walk side by side with his elders. He is not seeking progress, but wishes to become a grown-up man quickly.”

子曰:“恶紫之夺朱也,恶郑声之乱雅乐也,恶利口之覆邦家者。”

孔子说:“我厌恶那朱红的颜色被紫色所取代,我厌恶那雅正的音乐被那郑国的乐声破坏了,我厌恶那些卖弄口才扰乱家邦的人。”

Confucius said: “I dislike that the purple color takes away the luster of vermilion. I dislike that the music of Zheng takes away the elegant music. I dislike the people whose eloquent speech destroys the nation and its people.”

子曰:“予欲无言。”
子贡曰:“子如不言,则小子何述焉?”
子曰:“天何言哉。四时行焉,百物生焉,天何言哉!”

孔子说:“我不想再说话了。”
子贡说:“你如不说,那我们做弟子的还有什么可以传述的呢?”
孔子说:“老天也没有说话呀。然而四季照样运行,百物繁荣,天何曾说话呀!”

Confucius said: “I would rather not speak any more.”
Zi Gong said: “If you do not speak, how can we learn from you and teach others? ”
Confucius said: “The Heaven does not speak. Yet the four seasons still pursue their courses, and all things in nature grow up in time. The Heaven does not say anything! ”

孺悲欲见孔子,孔子辞以疾。将命者出户,取瑟而歌,使之闻之。

孺悲想见孔子,孔子不想见他,对传话的人说他生病了。可是,等传话的人刚走出去,孔子就拿起瑟来唱歌,故意让这个传话的人听到。

Ru Bei wished to visit Confucius. But Confucius didn' t want to receive Ru Bei and told his messenger that he was sick. Yet, as soon as the messenger stepped out, Confucius took his lute and sang in order to let the messenger hear.

子曰:“饱食终日,无所用心,难矣哉。不有博弈者乎?为之犹贤乎已。”

孔子说:“整天吃饱了什么用心的事也不做,是很难的呀。不是可以下棋吗?也比什么事都不做的好。”

Confucius said: “ It is hard for a man who eats all day and does nothing. Aren’ t there playing Chess? They would be better than not to do anything.”

齐景公待孔子,曰:“若季氏则吾不能,以季孟之闲待之。”曰:“吾老矣,不能用也。”孔子行。

齐景公想任用孔子,说:“如果我对待他像对待季氏一样,那是不可能的;我可以以对待季氏和孟氏中间的方式去对待他吧。”接着又说:“我老了,不能任用他了。”孔子听了以后就离开齐国了。

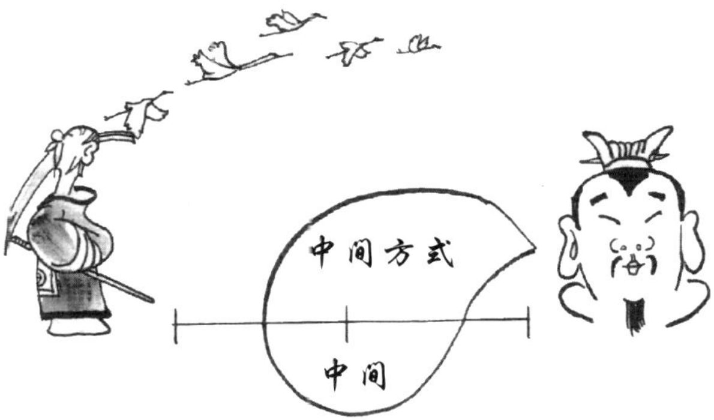


The Duke Jing of Qi was about to employ Confucius. He said to himself, “I can’t treat him the way I treated the chief of the Ji family. I am going to treat him the way between the two ways given to the chief of the Ji family and the chief of the Meng family.” Then the Duke added, “I am old. I can’t employ him.”
After hearing the saying, Confucius left the nation of Qi.

长沮桀溺耦而耕。孔子过之,使子路问津焉。
长沮曰:“夫执舆者为谁?”
子路曰:“为孔丘。”
曰:“是鲁孔丘与?”
曰:“是也。”
曰:“是知津矣。”
问于桀溺。桀溺曰:“子为谁?”
曰:“为仲由。”
曰:“是鲁孔丘之徒与?”
对曰:“然。”
曰:“滔滔者,天下皆是也。而谁以易之?且而与其从辟人之士也,岂若从辟世之士哉。”耰而不辍。
子路行以告。夫子怃然曰:“鸟兽不可与同群,吾非斯人之徒与而谁与?天下有道,丘不与易也。”

长沮和桀溺两人在田里耕作,孔子一行人经过,孔子要子路去问他们过河的渡口在哪儿。
长沮问:“在车上手执缰绳的人是谁?”
子路说:“是孔丘。”
长沮问:“是鲁国的那位孔丘吗?”
子路说:“是的。”
长沮说:“他应该知道渡口在哪儿的。”
子路又问桀溺渡口在哪儿。
桀溺说:“你是谁?”
子路说:“我是子路。”
桀溺问:“你是鲁国孔丘的弟子吗?”
子路说:“是的。”
桀溺说:“如今天下滔滔大乱,有谁能够把它改变过来?我看你与其跟着从一个国家去到另一个国家的那班人乱跑,还不如跟着我们这批避世隐居的人走的好。”
说罢,他仍旧继续耕他的田地而不再说话。
子路回去向孔子报告,孔子怃然叹道:“我既然不能和鸟类兽类合群,只有与人类为伍了。如果天下已经平治的话,那我也就用不着去寻求改革了。”

Chang Ju and Jie Ni were working in the field, when Confucius and his group walked by. Confucius wanted Zi Lu to ask them where a ford was .
Chang Ju asked: “Who is the man who holds the reins in the carriage? ”
Zi Lu said, “He is Confucius.”
Chang Ju asked, “Is that Confucius in Lu? ”
Zi Lu said, “Yes.”
Chang Ju then said, “He should know where the ford is.”
Zi Lu then asked the other man, Jie Ni, where a ford was.
Jie Ni asked, “Who are you? ”
Zi Lu said, “I am Zi Lu.”
Jie Ni asked, “Are you a disciple of Confucius in Lu? ”
Zi Lu said, “Yes.”
Jie Ni then said, “The whole world is in disorder. Who can make changes? It is better to follow those who are withdrawn from the world completely than to follow those who run from one nation to the other.”
Then he kept working in the field without saying any more.
Zi Lu reported the conversation to Confucius. Confucius heaved a heavy sign, saying: “Since I can not live in the world of the beasts and birds, I must live with the human beings without choice. If the world were in order, there would be no need for me to seek for changes.”

子路从而后,遇丈人以杖荷蓧。
子路问曰:"子见夫子乎?"
丈人曰:"四体不勤,五谷不分,孰为夫子?"
植其杖而芸,子路拱而立。止子路宿,杀鸡为黍而食之,见其二子焉。
明日,子路行以告。
子曰:"隐者也。"
使子路反见之。至则行矣。
子路曰:"不仕无义。长幼之节,不可废也。君臣之义,如之何其废之。欲洁其身,而乱大伦。君子之仕也,行其义也。道之不行,已知之矣。"

子路跟随孔子,落在后面,遇到了一位老人,用拐杖挑着竹筐子。
子路乃上前问道:"你看到我的老师没有?"
老人说:"手足都不劳动,恐怕连五谷也分不清楚,谁是你的老师?"
说完后就拿起拐杖到田里除草去了。子路拱着手站立,老人乃把子路带回家去住一宿,并杀鸡煮饭招待子路,又把他的两个儿子带来引见子路。

第二天，子路见到了孔子，他把经过情形向孔子报告。
孔子说："这是个隐者啊。"
孔子要子路回头再去拜访，子路到了老人家户，发现老人已经走了。
子路对老人家里的人传达孔子的话说："不替国家办事就是不尽责任。昨天老人引来他的两个儿子见我，那就是尽了长幼之间的礼节。老人家既已知道长幼之间的礼节不可废除，那君臣之间的礼节又怎么可以废除呢?老人家要清高，实际却乱了君臣之间的礼节。君子出来为政府服务，无非是尽点本分的责任而已。至于说他的政治理想能否实现，他也早已知道了的。"

Zi Lu, following his master, Confucius, fell behind. He met an old man who carried a basket for weeds on a staff over his shoulders. Zi Lu asked the old man: "Have you seen my master? "
The old man said: "You, folks, do not do any laboring works, do not know the toil. You can not tell the difference among five kinds of grain. Who is your master? "
Then he put his staff down and started to weed the ground. Zi Lu joined his hands across his breast and stood respectfully in waiting. The old man invited Zi Lu to his home to stay the night. He killed a chicken and prepared meal for Zi Lu. He also introduced his two sons to Zi Lu.
The next day, when Zi Lu caught up with Confucius, he told his master about the old man.
Confucius said: "He is a hermit."
And he sent Zi Lu back to see the old man, but the old man was gone.
Zi Lu told the old man's family what Confucius wanted him to say, "Not serving in the government is not performing his duty. Since he introduced his two sons to me yesterday, it means that he did not neglect the relationship between the old and the young. How could he neglect the relationship between the prince and him? He wants to maintain purity, but he neglects his duty to serve his prince. A superior man takes office in the government trying to perform his righteous duties. As for whether he could put his principles in progress, he has already known the answer."

子夏之门人问交于子张。
子张曰:“子夏云何?”
对曰:“子夏曰:‘可者与之,其不可者拒之。’”
子张曰:“异乎吾所闻。君子尊贤而容众,嘉善而矜不能。我之大贤与,于人何所不容。我之不贤与,人将拒我,如之何其拒人也。”

子夏的门人问子张如何交友。
子张问:“子夏怎么说?”
子夏的门人说:“子夏说,‘如果一个人可以接交,就和他做朋友;如不可以,就不要和他做朋友。’”
子张说:“这和我听到的不一样。君子尊重贤德的人,也容纳平庸的大众;嘉许善良的人,也要怜悯不善良的人。如果我是个贤德的人,当然会容纳所有的人;如果我不是贤德的人,别人将会拒绝我,我怎么能拒绝要和我做朋友的人呢?”

A disciple of Zi Xia asked Zi Zhang about the principle of friendship.
Zi Zhang asked what Zi Xia had told him about the subject.
The disciple said: “My master, Zi Xia, has taught me, ‘If a man can be made a friend, then make him a friend. Otherwise, do not make him a friend.’”
Zi Zhang said, “That is different from what I was taught. When a superior man honors the man of virtue, he is also tolerant of all other men. While he praises the man of virtue, he also pities the incompetent. If I am a man of virtue, I should be tolerant of all other men. If I am not, people will avoid me. How could I refuse those who want to be my friends?”

曾子曰:"吾闻诸夫子,'人未有自致者也,必也亲丧乎。'"

曾子说:"我听老师说过,'除了办理父母死亡的丧礼时,大凡一个人很少有事情是真正从内心里发出来的。"

Zeng Zi said: "I heard our master once said, 'Men do not do everything naturally and heartily. If they do, that must be when they are handling their parents' funerals.' "

子夏曰:"虽小道必有可观者焉。致远恐泥,是以君子不为也。"

子夏说:"虽然是很小的技艺可也有它的道理在,但如想集中心力在小的技艺上努力,还是成不了大事的。所以君子不肯在小的技艺上下功夫。"

Zi Xia said: " Even in the small and narrow branches of arts, there is something worthy. But if a man concentrates on the small and narrow branches of arts, he won't make achievement. Therefore, a superior man does not concentrate on the practice of small and narrow branch of arts."

子夏曰:“日知其所亡,月无忘其所能,可谓好学也已矣。”

子夏说:“每天知道一些所不知道的新知识,每月温习已经学到的知识,这个人可说是个好研究学问的人了。”

Zi Xia said: “If a man can learn something new every day, and review what he has learned every month, this man can surely be called a man who loves to learn.”

子夏曰:“百工居肆,以成其事。君子学以致其道。”

子夏说:“工匠在工地努力工作,才可以完成他的工艺;君子也必须努力学习,才可以达成大业。”

Zi Xia said: “A worker works in his shop in order to finish his products; likewise, a superior man keeps learning in order to reach his principles.”

子夏曰:“小人之过也,必文。”

子夏说:“小人犯了过失后,必定会去遮掩。”

Zi Xia said: “Whenever an inferior man is at fault, he would try to gloss over it.”

子夏曰:“君子有三变:望之俨然,即之也温,听其言也厉。”

子夏说:“君子的容态有三种变化:远远望去觉得很庄重,近看则很温和,听了他说话后,觉得他的话也很严正。”

Zi Xia said: “A superior man may be seen from three kinds of views. From a distance, he appears serious. In closer contact, he is kind. Listening to his speech, you will find his words are righteous.”

子游曰:“子夏之门人小子,当洒扫应对进退则可已,抑末也,本之则无。如之何?”
子夏闻之曰:“噫,言游过矣。君子之道,孰先传焉?孰后倦焉?譬诸草木,区以别矣。君子之道,焉可诬也。有始有卒者,其惟圣人乎。”

子游说:“子夏的门人弟子在厅堂里洒扫以及接待宾客进出等事情都可以说是做得很好了,不过这些都是末节不重要的,那最重要的根本学问却没有,这怎么可以呢?”
子夏听了后说:“子游的话说得太过了。君子的大道理,哪些应该先教?哪些可以放在后面教?这就好像去学习草木一样,区别很多,都要去学。君子之道,岂可以这么去乱教?至于说有始有终地教育学生,那只有圣人才可以如此啊。”

Zi You said: “Zi Xia’s disciples have learned good manners and deportment, yet they are but minor matters. They have not yet learned the important matters. How can that be?”
When Zi Xia heard this, he said: “Zi You is wrong. In education of the great principles, which must be taught first, and which must be taught second? It is like learning about the plants. We try to know all of them. How can the education of great principles be misdirected like this way? Only a sage can be smart enough to teach from the beginning till the end of principles without any problems.”

子夏曰:“仕而优则学。学而优则仕。”

子夏说:“服务政府如有余力,应当继续学习。学习充实了,就可以去服务政府了。”

Zi Xia said: “In serving in the government, if there are energies left, officials should keep learning new things. When a man has learned enough, he may go to serve in the government.”

子游曰:“丧,致乎哀而止。”

子游说:“参加丧礼时,能够尽了哀伤的心也就可以停止了。”

Zi You said: “ In the mourning process, whenever the heart-felt grief has been carried out, one may stop mourning.”

子游曰:“吾友张也,为难能也,然而未仁。”

子游说:“我的朋友子张能做很多事情,别人很难做到。虽然,他还没有达到仁者的境界。”

Zi You said: “My friend Zi Zhang can do many things which others can not perform. But he is still not yet a man of virtue.”

曾子曰:“堂堂乎张也!难与并为仁矣。”

曾子说:“子张相貌堂堂真是一表人材啊!很难与他一起进修仁道。”

Zeng Zi said: “How imposing Zi Zhang's manner is! It is hard to compare with him in practicing virtue.”

卫公孙朝问于子贡曰:“仲尼焉学?”
子贡曰:“文武之道,未坠于地,在人,贤者识其大者,不贤者识其小者,莫不有文武之道焉。夫子焉不学,而亦何常师之有。”

卫国公孙朝问子贡:“孔子的学问从哪里来的?”
子贡说:“文王和武王所遗留下来的道理,并没有完全遗失,仍留存在人们的心中,贤明的人记得重大的部分,不贤明的人记得那些较小的部分,到处仍有文王和武王的大道理在。我的老师无所不学,他根本没有一个固定的师承。”

Gongsun Chao of Wei asked Zi Gong where Confucius had learned all of his knowledge.
Zi Gong said: “ The doctrines of the Emperors of Wen and Wu times have not been forgotten completely. Some people still remember them. Men of talents and virtue remember the principles, and others remember the small things. So they all know the doctrines of the Emperors of Wen and Wu times. Our master learned from many people just about everywhere. He did not learn from only one particular teacher.”

叔孙武叔语大夫于朝曰:
“子贡贤于仲尼。”
子服景伯以告子贡。
子贡曰:“譬之宫墙,赐之墙也,及肩,窥见室家之好。夫子之墙数仞,不得其门而入,不见宗庙之美,百官之富。得其门者或寡矣。夫子之云,不亦宜乎。”

叔孙武叔在朝廷上对他的同僚说:“子贡的贤德超过他的老师孔子。”
子服景伯把这话告诉了子贡。
子贡说:“让我拿宫墙来做比喻吧。我的墙只有一个人的肩膀高,因此人们可以看见里面的美好;我老师的墙有数丈之高,假如人们找不到进去的门在哪儿,当然他们就看不到里面的珍宝。很不幸没有很多人能够找到门可以进入,所以叔孙武叔才会说那些不适宜的话。”

Officer Shusun Wushu said to the officials in the court: “Zi Gong is more superior than Confucius.”
Zifu Jingbo told Zi Gong this statement.
Zi Gong said: “Let me use the walls of a house as a comparison. I am like a wall which is as high as a man’s shoulder. People can see the beauty in the house while standing outside the wall. The wall of my master’s house is a hundred feet high. If people can not find a way to enter, they can not see the treasures inside the building. It is unfortunate that not many people can find the entrance to go inside. That may be the reason why Shusun Wushu made that unsuitable statement.”

叔孙武叔毁仲尼。
子贡曰:“无以为也,仲尼不可毁也。他人之贤者,丘陵也,犹可逾也;仲尼,日月也,无得而逾焉。人虽欲自绝,其何伤于日月乎,多见其不知量也。”

叔孙武叔毁谤仲尼(孔子)。
子贡说:“这是不可以的。仲尼是不可以毁谤的。一般所谓贤德的人,就像一座丘陵一样,人还是可以攀越的。仲尼可像日月一样,人是无法攀越的。即使有人想要自绝于日月,这对日月仍是毫无伤害的,只能表示出你是自不量力而已。”

Shusun Wushu reviled Confucius.
Zi Gong said: “Do not do that. Confucius can not be reviled. The virtue of other men is but like hillocks which can still be stepped over. Confucius’s virtue is like the sun or the moon. Nobody can step over the sun or the moon. Even if a person wants to cut himself off from the sun and the moon, there is no harm to the sun or the moon. It only proves that you don’t know your own ability.”

陈子禽谓子贡曰:“子为恭也,仲尼岂贤于子乎?”
子贡曰:“君子一言以为知,一言以为不知,言不可不慎也。夫子之不可及也,犹天之不可阶而升也。夫子之得邦家者,所谓立之斯立,道之斯行,绥之斯来,动之斯和。其生也荣,其死也哀,如之何其可及也?”

陈子禽对子贡说:“你不过是恭敬仲尼罢了,仲尼哪里有你贤德呢?”
子贡说:“君子的一句话可以显出是聪明,一句话也可以显出是不聪明。所以君子说话要慎重啊。我的老师之不可以比得上,就好像不可以乘梯子上天一样。假如我的老师可以执掌政权,那就像古语所说的如要使人民生计能够自立,就能自立,教化盛行,人民归附,一片祥和,老师不仅活着光荣,死后人们也将尽哀。我如何可以赶得上老师呢?”

Chen Zi Qin said to Zi Gong: “You are too modest. How can Confucius be more superior than you? ”

Zi Gong said: “ A superior man can be judged if he is smart or not by only one word. Therefore, a superior man ought to be careful when he speaks. Our master can not be equaled just as the Heaven can not be reached by a stairway. Had our master been in the position of a ruler in a state, he would have made the people live comfortably, the right principles would have prevailed, the people would have moved in from faraway, and the society would have been peaceful. Our master not only lives in glor, but also will be sorrowed by people after his death. How could I equal to my master? ”